"LEAVE WHITE FOLKS ALONE!"

By: Donnie A. Hyder Sr.

Copyright © 2008 by Donnie A. Hyder, Sr.

Wyndham House Publishers, Inc.

ISBN 10: 0-615-22904-2
ISBN 13: 978-0-615-22904-1

This book is dedicated to my amazing wife, Selma W. Hyder, who has stuck by my side all these years and through unbelievably challenging circumstances much of the time. Her unconditional love and support was monumental in bringing this work to fruition.

Thank you Sweetheart!

INTRODUCTION

This book is fundamentally a conversation with America as a whole from a perspective it is certainly not used to. It is purposed to engage Whites with open and honest dialogue regarding Race Relations but more importantly, be an inspirational and educational gift to Blacks and other minorities in the United States Of America who desire to share in the American Dream. I trust and expect that it will speak to the affluent, political giants, legislators, elitists, red necks, sexists and racists alike.

This book is sure to speak truth to all of my countrymen in the true spirit of patriotism as I truly do love and appreciate all that America is and will be. Everyone's not going to agree with my every position including Blacks even down to my family and immediate household. Nonetheless I am committed to speak the truth relentlessly regardless of who might oppose it.

On purpose, I refused to speak to literary consultants on how best to write this book. I purposely did not reach out to any editors or publishing companies to find out if they would be interested in my message or even if they thought there was such an audience that would be amenable. Instead I decided to pen my thoughts collectively in their purest form and demand that America, but more importantly my people, hear the message that has been stirring in me for decades. The time is now and I am certain that this book will inspire Americans and all people to be better - but especially my people. . .The Black Race!

TABLE OF CONTENTS

CHAPTER ONE	CHEAPER TO BE WHITE THAN BLACK	1
CHAPTER TWO	THE BATTLE OF THE MIND	31
CHAPTER THREE	LET BY GONES BE BY GONES	51
CHAPTER FOUR	DIAMONDS IN THE ROUGH	65
CHAPTER FIVE	BLACK FOLKS ONLY SECTION	93
CHAPTER SIX	THE DIFFERENCE BETWEEN THE RICH AND POOR	143
CHAPTER SEVEN	THE POWER OF A 700 FICO SCORE	195
CHAPTER EIGHT	FOUR METHODS OF PRODUCING MONEY	213
CHAPTER NINE	$50K A YEAR INCOME GUARANTEED FOR ALL	235
CHAPTER TEN	PRESIDENT BARACK OBAMA	263

CHAPTER 1

"IT'S CHEAPER TO BE WHITE THAN BLACK!"

Let me start by expressing the fact that I truly believe that America is the greatest country on the planet and that I absolutely adore it. I'd rather claim no other dwelling as home this side of heaven. That's right, I'm not an angry Black man trying to move back to Africa.

Moreover, I want to make it just as lucid that I positively love WHITE people. This preface is so significant as it is certain that many will attempt to characterize and demonize this book as racist, leftist and their favorite one of all. . . unpatriotic. You will discover, however it is just the opposite.

I know one of the first questions people will ask is, "Who in the world is this young Black dude writing to mainstream America and the Black community therein? By what authority does he write it? And what makes him think ANYBODY cares or gives a dog gone what he thinks?" I think those are fair questions that even I would probably like answered if I were on the other side of this book considering whether or not it is a worthy read, let alone embrace its philosophies. It is important to note that despite the fact I will be sharing a lot of my story, this book is not about me.

Well just to get us started, I represent some of the worst and the best of Blacks in America. I am 35 years old and have spent 7 of the best of those years incarcerated in North Carolina's penitentiary, being committed in 1991. Going back as far as I can remember as a child at the age of 4 years old, I remember my family living in what is known as Debry projects in a small town in North Carolina. Notice I said my

FAMILY lived there which consisted of my Mom, Dad, brother and sister - so it wasn't quite as bad as one might think when you think of a guy from the projects. A family consisting of both the Mom and the Dad in the house is a luxury that kids who grow up that way just take for granted. Trust me it is a LUXURY worth more than money can buy.

Nonetheless, by age 7 my world was shattered by my parents' sudden (at least sudden to me) divorce. In grade school, I was always among the brightest in my class. You name it - straight A's, perfect attendance, best school projects, spelling bee champ, class president and all. Oh, and I of course was the one who was called upon to deliver all the important speeches on behalf of the student body. I was the Speech King and the apple of my parents' eyes. I was different – a leader and trend setter. You know, I was a pretty bright kid and good looking, I thought - full of self esteem.

Hey, Dad landed a good job in Atlanta early on, bought a cozy brick home and moved us there at age 5 just in time for me to make my kindergarten debut. I remember vividly wearing three piece suits to school because my Dad told me that I was gonna be a successful lawyer or business man and take care of him one day. I never forgot the positive words my Mom and Dad spoke into my life at that early age – my teachers, too. During all that time, I cannot remember a single time where I heard my Mom and Dad fight or cuss. Almost at once, however, the divorce was announced and Dad was moving over 600 miles away back to North Carolina. Go figure!

From that time on, my brother and I moved back and forth between North Carolina and Atlanta - one year with Mom, the next with Dad. I didn't manage to get over my parents divorce until I was actually grown and in prison. I rebelled in so many different ways that I'm embarrassed to name even a few of them. Americans who grow up with both parents in the home cannot begin to imagine how fortunate they really are. And children who grow up in one parent homes never having experienced at all what it's like to have a Daddy in the home have no idea what they are deprived of. However psychologically to a young kid who has experienced it and suddenly have it snatched away without any warning, is a devastating event that only those who've experienced it can fathom.

Despite my intellectual advantages, it is still amazing to me and consequently so very embarrassing to reflect on the fact that I never graduated from High School. But worse than that, can you believe that I actually flunked the 11th grade? Come on now, both my Mom and my Dad are college graduates and I'm a straight A student. How do I flunk the 11th grade? As far as I'm aware, my Mom doesn't know that to this very day as I certainly never had the guts to tell her. After all, my Mom was an accomplished Honors English teacher at the time. Education and its importance was something she was very passionate about. She would be devastated not that she wasn't already regarding the other revelations.

I was living with my Dad back in North Carolina the school year that I flunked, and went to school the next year pretending like I was in twelfth grade. I was so embarrassed. My Dad knew but I had everybody else fooled – at least I thought I did. That is, until Clarissa

Allen, one of my classmates asked me what grade I was in. Now we've been in the same doggone grade every since we've known each other and she's gonna ask a brother what grade he's in. DOG! Of course at this point I'm miserable because if she knows, then so does everyone else.

Now you know I absolutely HATED school at this juncture especially since I used to brag about my grades and the fact that I didn't have to study much at all and could still ACE tests. Didn't do any homework in those days but I could Ace any test and run circles around the smartest of girls in my class. Ask D.D. and Telonna – they'll tell you. No, ask Mrs. Thompson - my Honors English Teacher. Yes, I was taking Honors English the year I flunked. How does that happen?

Just when I thought things could not get any worse, my life took a dramatic turn that whereas I took for granted that I'd be in homeroom class the next morning, something terrible happened the night before in which I found myself in the county jail without bond charged with first degree murder and facing a life sentence. This couldn't be happening. Certainly, I didn't kill anybody. I remember thinking to myself, "I've got class in the morning – I've gotta get out of here. But a brother wasn't going no where!

Seventeen years old, eleventh grade with a first degree murder charge, and on the front page of the local newspaper! By the way, the murder charge was dropped as I was only charged because I was among those present at the scene. It didn't help that two eye witnesses swore that it was me who was the shooter. Although authorities were certain it wasn't me very shortly thereafter, it still took over a year to get the charges dropped. I was in prison serving 7 years of a 25 year sentence from a previous charge when this was accomplished. The adjudication of the pending charge allowed my prison status to be reduced from close custody to medium which dropped me down a couple of floors in that 17 story High Rise prison that I was housed.

Oh, I failed to mention that I had a new baby on the way in the midst of it all and my soon to be baby's momma (Tracey) was only 15 and grew up without her father in the home as well. So let's be clear here. I'm 17 years old, just flunked the 11th grade, caught a murder charge with no bond, and got a baby on the way by a 15 year old who's gonna bring a child in the world with no hopes of a father in the home just like for most of my conscious childhood years and all of Tracey's. Therefore, I'm starting a 25 year bid straight out of the 11th grade - a quarter century – stuff that 50 Cent was rapping about in "21 Questions." Except in my case, it was for real.

Does the cycle sound familiar at all? What else could possibly go wrong? Trust me there is plenty more. But I'll get into that much later. Just wanted to establish the fact that I'm qualified to speak to this cause. By no means am I proud to be because I assure you, I would rather have subscribed to the straight and narrow and avoided the heartache and pain that goes along with my story. And I am not suggesting that something "happened to me" - no doubt the choices that I made are the reasons I found myself there. No excuses. Nonetheless my aim is to shed light on the plight that all too often Black men and women find themselves gravitating toward without even realizing it until they are there and it seems hopelessly too late. Please note that I said that it SEEMS too late. But quite the contrary, I am evidence that it is never too late. My goal though is to thwart this negative cycle by promotion of knowledge and waking us up to the reality of what a very bright and valuable people we are – because we truly are.

Everyone knows somebody who is or was just like me whether a son or daughter, cousin, nephew, niece, grandson or daughter, student or kid in the neighborhood. In fact, I am certain that most cases will NOT be as extreme as mine so if I can overcome it, everyone can. Most people couldn't get into the kind of trouble I was in if they tried to on purpose. Actually when I caught the 25 year bid (could have got 40 years which was the max for that charge), I was still facing a Life Sentence for the pending murder charge. Therefore, at one point during what was supposed to be my senior year in High School, I was facing Life plus 40 years. So let me see:

1. Broken Home at early age
2. Projects
3. Murder Charge
4. Exposed To Drug Dealing
5. Premarital sex
6. Baby On The Way
7. 5 Year Bid Facing Life
8. Guns And Drugs
9. Flunked 11th Grade
10. Black

Only things I see missing from this list that I did not experience or witness was child molestation and domestic violence in the home. I do have dear friends of mine who have endured the latter but thankfully, they too survived. Nevertheless, my point is that not many people are going to encounter MORE than my share of misfortunes at such an early age. They may experience various elements on smaller scales and then maybe later on in life they aggregate to equal or greater, but you have to admit that that's a tough pill for anyone to swallow or survive, let alone overcome and rise above.

I'd like to think that I did overcome it. As I write today, I am not writing from in prison nor am I on Parole. As far as I know, I don't have any charges pending and while I'm not what I consider rich, I think I live a pretty comfortable lifestyle with my wife and 5 children. And yes, I managed to emerge with my sanity intact though some might beg to disagree with that overall characterization.

But please do not misunderstand me. I do not share my story to gain any sympathy from anyone subscribing to this writing. Though I am a very humble and thankful person, I am as self confident and articulate as the guy who has never given the world a minute's trouble and boasts an MBA from Harvard or Princeton Universities. I understand and appreciate the fact that America is very tolerable and it's so amazing that any and everybody from any walk of life can rise above their circumstances and be successful in life.

I literally believe that I could be President of the United States if I so chose to. I currently conduct business with dignitaries on levels that would intimidate the sharpest executives and statesmen. I am privileged to travel for the most part by private airplane and have been driving S Class Mercedes since the 90's, before they were assessable to ordinary consumers. So please by no means should anyone feel sorry for me.

Having sampled everything from auto-detailing (washing cars) to my current trade which happens to be real-estate investing, I have learned a few things that many might find useful in the struggle to rise above poverty and share in the American Dream. Through entrepreneurship, I have had the privilege of generating and controlling millions of dollars over the years. I have messed up more money than most people will ever see in a lifetime. Likewise I have broken more barriers and achieved more success than many will ever achieve, but have failed far more times than I have succeeded and have the bumps and bruises to prove it. Having done so, I believe I bring to the table a wealth of knowledge that readers will find unique compared to the kind of people who write these types of books.

Traditionally the guys who write these types of books are either White guys who come from suburban well to do families or White guys who were poor but were able to learn the ropes from the school of hard knocks and rise to affluence. I would have considered either a head start from where I and most other Blacks who have such aspirations have to begin. I would be ecstatic to have Robert Kiyosaki's poor dad be my rich dad. And to grow up as Donald Trump did with the benefit of his father and other colleagues mentoring him every step of the way in the real estate industry would have been a dream come true. I'm not knocking these guys as I am among their biggest fans and have learned a great deal from them both. I appreciate them immensely.

But believe it or not, there's a difference between the road to success for a Black business man coming up through the ranks than his White counterparts. There is a different set of rules, different standards, different expectations and it is important to understand those differences. I'm not complaining or whining about them – my goal is merely to dispel the myths and false hopes that are all too often sold by America that these differences do not exist. I can hear elitist saying, "Here goes another guy that's gonna give us 40 excuses why Black people can't make it in America." But stay with me, I assure you that that's clearly not where I am headed.

Remember, I believe that this is the greatest country in the world today and I am very proud to be an American. Try to ship me back to Africa or elsewhere out of the country and I'll be kicking and screaming trying to stay. So please don't misunderstand me. Nonetheless, it is a fact that in this country it is indeed CHEAPER TO BE WHITE than Black, or Hispanic, or even Jew.

I realize that America doesn't necessarily want to have this discussion. It's actually getting to the point where Whites in this country are embarrassed by it because it's so obvious. But the good news is that there is a shift taking place that is so subtle but so widespread that no intelligent person observing can deny it. A very good example of this is what has taken place during the presidential primaries, more particularly the Barack Obama Campaign. Mainstream America was blown away by the overwhelming support that White upper classed Iowans gave to a young Black guy, new on the scene. It took America by storm and it continues to do so today even though the status quo has fought it tenaciously.

Thanks to the blood and sweat of our forefathers along with the persistence of the mighty warriors we have on the front lines of the battlefield of justice today, Blacks have made tremendous strides of advancement in this country. We've excelled on nearly every front and are waxing stronger and stronger. One area, however, that we have failed miserably in is our understanding and application of economics.

According to Georgia University's Selig Center, Blacks in America have the combined spending power (2007) of over 845 Billion dollars. Trouble with those figures are that although they are pretty significant, they tend to yield very little return as it relates to our cultural power and leverage as a collective group. It's not very smart to me that we pump nearly a trillion dollars into this economy yet do not enjoy our fair share of dominance with regard to wealth. Now when I speak of dominance in wealth, I'm not talking about Cadillacs, Rims and Gold teeth - or even $350,000 homes in the suburbs or S 500 Mercedes or Bentleys.

When I talk about wealth dominance, I wanna know how many Black Owned banks we have and mainstream like a Suntrust or Bank of America with locations nationally? I'm interested in how many - or if we have any at all - major television networks we own or control? What I'd like to know is how many mainstream insurance companies we own or control? It would interest me to discover how many brokerage firms are owned by Blacks in America or how many hotel chains, resorts, and skyscrapers we have adorning New York City's skyline?

Do we own any Gulfstream jets that we can send to Louisiana to pick up our loved ones during a crisis instead of complaining about what former President George Bush is gonna do or (not do) about it? The point I am making is that in my opinion we have become complacent with each of us individually owning a nice house, a nice automobile, and having a good job earning $100,000 a year (between 2 wage earners).

I must admit that even that is a great improvement from being a slave and having none of the latter luxuries mentioned above. And I can hear elitest and (for lack of a better term) Uncle Tom Blacks counseling, "What are you complaining about- you've got it better than you ever have – this line of thinking is just materialistic and serves only to divide." However, it just seems that every time someone stands up to try to motivate and challenge Black people to achieve greater things such as EQUALITY economically, what I call the DIVISION CARD is played.

"You know America is ONE and there is no Black, White, Hispanic etc. We are all ONE in the spirit." This is the curtain that upper classed White America has been hiding behind for decades and persecuting anybody that would oppose it. But what I see it as is nothing but manipulation and exploitation of the sheer ignorance of

Blacks as it relates to Economic Empowerment. We are made to feel unpatriotic when we esteem ourselves or make a conscious unified effort to advance ourselves. We are deceived as we were during slavery times when the master made basic concessions like allowing us to go to church while forbidding us to learn to read and write. We were coached by the elders and Uncle Toms to feel guilty about desiring and attempting to learn to read and write because the master was "doing good by us" in letting us go to church.

The same manipulation and exploitation is going on today but I submit to you that it's not the master's fault this time, as we know better. It's not the White man's fault this time – we're FREE! As powerful as it was and is, the Emancipation Proclamation and the great Constitution of these United States of America does not guarantee or create financial dominance or independence. They merely provide us the opportunity or CHANCE to make it happen for ourselves.

The ignorance of Black people in America regarding economics taxes significantly our progress in reaching our goals of economic empowerment and equality, thus making it even more expensive to be Black than White in America. I would have to estimate that 95 percent of Blacks don't operate with the benefit of this reality, especially the middle to upper class. Again, this is not a divisive message but an informative one and a discussion that America needs to engage open-mindedly if it is ever to change. But more importantly, it is a discussion that Blacks in America must engage and effectively employ solutions and corrective measures to eliminate the problem both individually and collectively.

WHITE PEOPLE...

When America's judges are White it's to your advantage.
When America's lawyers are White it's to your advantage.
When America's policemen are White, it's to your advantage.
When America's congressmen are White it's to you're advantage.
When America's news networks are White it's to your advantage.
When America's landlords are White it's to your advantage.
When America's bankers are White it's to your advantage.
When America's clerks of court are White it's to your advantage.
When America's federal agents are White it's to your advantage.

Now I wanna know who would be so bold as to challenge the truths set forth above. Or who would dare stand up and have the audacity to declare that it is just not true. What intellectual would dare engage the Black community in this debate? It would be futile and utterly a lost cause as there would be no sustainable facts to support an argument to the contrary. It's just plain cheaper to be **"White"** than Black in America.

Everybody calm down, take a deep breath, and let it sink in. I realize it's difficult and uncomfortable but let's everyone digest it. It's good for us to have this discussion as unseemly as it may be - America is ready to have this conversation.

Usually the first, natural reaction White people have when forced to confront such realities would be to emphatically deny the accuracy of statements like that and offer that we as Blacks are merely making excuses for why we haven't achieved greater success. For many, it is actually very embarrassing when they truly think about and realize that Blacks really are at a disadvantage economically and socially in the U.S. Others on the other hand, simply choose to refuse to accept it as so and attempt to convince themselves and others around them that the playing field is in fact level – that there is only an appearance of an advantage. In other words, it's just a mind thing.

Look, I am not in any way suggesting in this book that White people should be ashamed or embarrassed about the reality that they have an obvious advantage economically in this country. In fact, I don't think it's necessarily their fault at this point or for that matter their problem. My goal is to educate and enlighten more so Blacks who have bought into the lie that the costs are the same. There is nothing worse than being deceived about a thing when everybody around us knows the truth and we're the only one who can't figure out why we keep coming up with the short end of the stick.

African Americans need to understand that the cost of living for us in the United States is higher than that of our White counterparts. I'm not suggesting that it's right or wrong per se. I am merely bringing awareness to its reality so that change can be effected. The "overhead," if you will, of the typical Black family is significantly higher than that of the White family with substantially the same make up.

Take two single guys fresh on the scene - one White and the other Black. Both are college graduates with degrees in Computer Science first year out of school. White guy's name is Tommy and Black guy's name Eric. Both have 700 Fico scores and just bought identical homes across the street from each other in a decent neighborhood.

Tommy's Dad happens to be acquainted with a senior-level executive at Bellsouth who at the request of his Dad offers Tommy an entry level job as an I.T. tech straight out of school. Three months later Tommy finds the 3 bedroom 2 bath bungalow he loves for $120,000. Fortunately, Tommy's uncle went to college with the local loan officer at Suntrust Bank and gives Tommy a good reference which along with his pretty good credit score lands him a first time buyer's mortgage, despite the fact that he has a very limited credit history.

Because the loan officer promised Tommy's Uncle that he would take good care of his nephew, the Suntrust banker offers Tommy the bank's $0 closing cost option even though Tommy is unable to appreciate its significance, being "green" to the mortgage process. Typical closing costs on a $120,000 mortgage could easily top $3,500 or more. Moreover while a fair mortgage rate would have been about 7.5% APR at the time, the loan officer only holds a point of rate thus shaving Tommy's rate to 6.5%. A one percent rate reduction on a $120,000.00 mortgage reduces a payment by about $122.00 per month and saves about $44,000.00 over a 30 year period. Tommy's monthly payment (not including taxes and insurance) would equal about $758.48.

Within a 12 month period Tommy has found favor with management at Bellsouth and has been promoted to assistant manager which boosted his income to $65,000 and as you can see is well on his way up the corporate ladder. I don't have to tell you that 97% of senior level executives at major corporations are White across the board. Hey I'm not complaining here but simply educating. It's a fact and we know how politics goes – senior executives pull up guys from the bottom that they know and like. They promote their buddies and their buddy's buddies. Trouble is, they don't generally have any Black buddies.

Therefore a lot of times we cry racism and discrimination where in all fairness, it is oftentimes not. You see, it's simply just that these high level executives, lawyers, bankers, and judges just don't hang out with Black Folks. Can you dig it? And executives generally don't hire people they don't know or aren't familiar with. Anyway, that's just how it is.

Eric, too, is optimistic about landing a job fresh out of school and sets out to make it happen as well, full of vigor. He diligently applies at Sprint, Verizon, as well as Bellsouth, but discovers that while he interviews well, there seems to be no openings available at the time. Eric doesn't stop there of course but continues to seek employment with smaller companies and in the meantime lands a part time gig making $12.00 an hour at a local library, but is still hopeful that something better will come through. For the next 4 months, Eric would reapply or update his applications with the same major companies until finally because of his persistence, one agrees to give him a shot. Eric is ecstatic and making a whopping $45,000 a year to start at Bellsouth with his future looking brighter than ever.

Like Tommy, Eric finds a nice home for $120,000 (in the same neighborhood) that he aspires to purchase and goes down to the local Suntrust which is not far from the house and applies for a mortgage. Just so happens that he runs into the same loan officer that went to school with Tommy's Uncle. After careful review of Eric's application, the loan officer informs Eric that although he had a pretty decent credit score, the bank was unable to approve his loan at the time citing limited credit history, and short time on the job. Eric is not about to give up there, however. He goes to the next bank down the street but learns that they are unwilling to grant him the loan as well. Eric continues to apply with 3 additional banks in the city and achieves the same result from each, with reasons varying from not enough time of job to needing a cosigner. The real reason, I submit, is that neither he nor his family knows anybody in banking and nobody knows them.

Finally though, one of the loan officers gives him a break by referring Eric to one of his mortgage-broker friends where Eric is finally approved! Eric is on top of the world at the news that he will be getting his first house. Only it is 6 months later and the market has changed where prices have gone up a bit. Of course the original home he was looking at had already sold for the $120,000 asking price. But luckily there was another one that came on the market across the street from

Tommy but it was listed at the appreciated price of $135,000. Still, it was worth it.

The mortgage broker informed Eric that while he had a pretty decent credit score, because of his limited credit history in addition to short time on the job that his rate would be a higher 8.99% and closing costs would be a little steep as well to the tune of $4,500. Good thing Eric was pretty good with his money and had saved a good amount instead of wasting it during the past few months. He had more than enough to cover the upfront closing costs and reserves as well.

Eric would learn further that the mortgage company that had agreed to extend him the loan required as a condition of the loan that he pay mortgage insurance. It was not required with Tommy's loan being a primary loan with Suntrust, a primary lender. Most secondary or sub-prime lenders require mortgage insurance automatically when the loan to value exceeds 90%. In Eric's case, Mortgage insurance (M.I.) added about $154.64 to his already hefty $1,085.00 (not including escrow for taxes and insurance) which brought his total payment to $1,239.64.

Let's contrast the two individuals only a year into the world grown and on their own.

Tommy (White)   **Eric (Black)**

1. Bellsouth I.T Tech $50,000   Bellsouth I.T. $45,000
   *Lands job fresh out of school   *Lands job 4 months out of school
   *Promotion and $15K Raise   * $2,000 Raise After 12 Months
   After 12 Months

*It is estimated that the Salary/Promotion contrast between Whites and Blacks over any sustained period being conservative equates to a minimum of $25,000 annually across the board. $25k X Just 10 years = a whooping $250,000.00

2. Purchases Home   120,000.00   135,000.00

3. Equity in Property $15,000   Equity $0

4. Primary Mortgage   6.5%   Sub-Prime   8.99%

5. No Mortgage Insurance Required   Mortgage Insurance $154.64

6. Monthly Payment $758.48   Monthly Payment $1,239.64

7. Payments over term $273,052.80   Payments over term = $446,270.40

After examining the above outline carefully, there can be no doubt whatsoever that Tommy who is White has a major advantage economically over his counterpart Eric who happens to be African American. Now nobody's suggesting here that somehow it is Tommy's fault that he's in a better position financially or even that it's Tommy's Dad or family's fault. No implication here that RACISM played a part or that Eric was a victim of discrimination. In fact, I will go as far to declare emphatically that there was No discrimination involved and that neither Tommy nor Eric did anything wrong but simply maximized the benefits and opportunities afforded to each.

Both Tommy and Eric were responsible young men who graduated from the same school at the same time. Neither were lazy nor complacent but innovative and full of excitement and confidence. Both were responsible and maintained very good credit, though obviously limited and both took advantage of the opportunities that were available to them. No one could possibly fault Eric simply because neither he nor his family knew intimately a senior level manager at Bellsouth who could open doors internally as Tommy's Dad did. The fact is there is a scarcity of Blacks in senior management in corporations and banks nationally and absolutely none in the town that they lived in. The chances that Eric, as is the case with many young Blacks, would have a Black banker in position that might look favorably upon his situation and make the decision to grant him a primary mortgage through the local bank was slim to none.

I freely admit that Eric's profile probably did not merit the loan on his own at that stage of his life fresh out of school, new on the job, and with very short credit history. But, neither did Tommy's. It was only because there was common familiarity with the loan officer and a close Uncle of Tommy's that made that possible.

The loan officer basically went out on a limb (which was in his discretion) and took a chance with Tommy being impressed with his progress so far, admittedly - not JUST because of the Uncle. But mind you, he was just as impressed with Eric however, the common denominator is missing - the (White) Uncle or the familiarity. This is just a luxury that Whites enjoy over Blacks. There were just no African American loan officers in their city with lending authority, as is the case in the vast majority of cities in America at this time. Certainly there are some somewhere with lending authority but poll them and I will guarantee there are less than 3% across the board. Poll the banks and see for yourself.

Now I must admit that I have seen a wave of Black branch managers emerging across the country in an attempt to appear to have Black loan officers but they have absolutely NO lending authority whatsoever. They can open savings and checking accounts, take applications to be reviewed and decided by REAL loan officers, ok the early clearing of a couple small checks that HOLDS could have been put upon for 3 to 5 days, but that's it. These guys can't make an independent decision on a $5,000.00 car loan to a brother who has a 760 FICO score, earns $100k a year income and no debt.

Problem is, Tommy doesn't even realize that he has benefited from this reality or that he shares any type of advantage whatsoever over his Black peers. This is why whenever African Americans engage in the debate over these issues, more often than not White people deny very passionately the notion that the deck is stacked in their favor. Therefore many are sincere when making their arguments to the contrary. Despite that sincerity however, it truly IS Cheaper to Be White than Black in America. Like Bernie Mac says, "Right or Wrong?"

What's worse to me than Tommy not knowing, (because what do you want Tommy to do, not take the loan or not take the job), is the fact that Eric doesn't know. It's not so much that Tommy or White people are "to do something" as much as it is that Eric and Black people tend to "do nothing" because of ignorance of these truths. Eric assumes that there exists no advantage among his White peers, which in and of itself is a disadvantage and produces two major negative results.

1. Eric may wrongfully conclude because of his ignorance that somehow Tommy is superior OR at least sharper than he is and subconsciously accept that subservient role henceforth not realizing the need to bridge the gap. Eric remains lopsided and it translates to millions over a lifetime. Self esteem, self worth and lifetime achievement potential are all at stake.

2. Generations (our precious sons) of African Americans fall further and further behind prolonging the struggle needlessly. We don't study to catch up because we aren't aware that we're behind. We take recess when everybody else does. Like in The Tortoise and The Hare, the Tortoise had sense

enough to know he had to keep moving and we would be wise to do likewise.

None can deny that we as a people have come a mighty long way since slavery thanks to patriarchs like Dr. Martin Luther King, Jr. and many other mighty warriors of the cause. However there is a long road ahead and much work to be done. I am a strong advocate of educating our people of the realities that confront us every day and my approach is not to whine and complain to White people about them but to take steps and leaps forward that will close the gaps and advance African Americans from within. We must identify where we are weak and lacking and launch a formidable offensive that will eradicate those barriers that constrain us.

I encourage everyone reading this book to take the time to carefully examine Tommy and Eric in the previous analogy as it is a very practical one that all of us, if we're honest with ourselves, would have to agree is as close to real as we can get. I am not going to bother explaining in detail any further the disparities that are obvious therein other than to remark that being conservative, I have no reservations whatsoever in declaring that it costs a professional at least an extra $1,000,000.00 to be Black in America than it does to be White, over a lifetime.

Keep in mind now we are talking about the professional Negro that has done everything right. This is the guy with a RELEVANT (to today's economy) education. He's responsible with his finances, maintains a 700+ Fico score - a very bright, hard working fellow. This is not the guy that parties all the time and is susceptible to getting in trouble with the law or has 2 or 3 Baby's Mommas, to all of which he is obligated to divide his income. This guy is financially literate, on the ball, and is well on his way to attaining the American Dream.

It wearies me to even think of beginning the task of tallying up the costs of the guy who is the opposite. By the time you factor in a lifetime of late fees, making bond, hiring defense attorneys, bad credit scores, denial of benefits that having good credit affords, a lifetime of renting apartments, and host of other things – I would guess that it could easily cost this guy about 3 to 5 million over a lifetime. This really doesn't count in the equation because this guy's disadvantage is self inflicted, though also attributable to his ignorance.

Either way, it's not the White man's fault. Ultimately whether you're the guy that's doing everything right (that he knows to do at this point) or the one adding additional obstacles himself, we still have to take responsibility for where we are now and take control of where we are going. This is true individually as well as collectively as a people.

If you are running a marathon and you are aware that your opponent has been clocking better times than you, you'd better study and discover why. Are they faster? Do they have better endurance? Are they mentally stronger than you or what? Maybe you will find that they have been clocked at those impressive times while running downhill whereas you were timed on flatland or slightly uphill. It could be that the distance measured was inaccurate or the times keeper was off. Whatever the reason, if you expect to compete or even have a reasonable chance of prevailing, it would behoove you to at least find out why your results are substandard to those of your competitor's. You have gotta know what you're up against, as knowing is half the battle. It's only once you have gained knowledge of truth can you ever have hope of changing your circumstances and ultimately overcoming your obstacles. Ignorance is not a virtue.

Just so we're clear….

It is to our advantage to make sure we demand adequate representation in our court systems by electing Black Judges to the bench. We do this by lobbying Black lawyers encouraging and financially supporting their campaigns for Judge's seats.

It is to our advantage to elect Black district attorneys to represent our counties. After all, these are the guys prosecuting our children and community. Trust me, it is to our advantage but we as a people don't even consider running for this office. Again, we are ignorant of District Attorneys' impact on our community. It is a powerful position that we give away every election. We don't even try in most instances. In most cases, the District Attorney doesn't even ask for our votes or come before us to address our issues. He has a FREE pass while enjoying unchallenged discretion and authority over our children. It is to White people's advantage to have White District Attorneys. Certainly they will be more sensitive to the needs of their White counterparts, comrades, high school buddies and friends moreso than to Blacks who they are not personally acquainted with and who make no demands of them.

It is to our advantage to make sure we demand that banks put African American loan officers and underwriters with lending authority in our local branch offices. We accomplish this by encouraging Black professionals in the banking field to ask for these positions and sign petitions to be presented to board members regarding these concerns. They have to listen and will respond. But guess what, nobody's asked.

It is to our advantage to elect African Americans to City Council, State Senate and House of Representative positions to represent our communities on the local, state, and federal levels of government. After all, the laws being passed and decisions being made on all levels directly affect our well being in society. We weren't present or adequately represented when the Rockefeller Drug laws were passed in New York and we see the years, sweat, and tears it has taken to reverse those unfair laws targeting our young Black youth. The time just does not fit the crime and they know it but this is what happens when we are not adequately represented. We change things and prevent it from happening again in the future by getting involved with politics and getting our representatives into office. Period.

It is to our advantage to purpose to make these adjustments and many more in this country for in doing so we shave hundreds of thousands of dollars off the "Black Tax" - the hidden uncontroverted tax that Blacks pay everyday in America. We significantly reduce these taxes and costs not by lobbying congress, the president, or begging White people to do something for us, but by being informed and being proactive about enacting the changes suggested in this chapter ourselves. I am not saying that it will be completely eliminated but I am declaring that it can be drastically reduced. Together by joining a concentrated effort to implement these initiatives, we can internally pass a bill that will produce the greatest Tax Cut this country has ever seen. I like to refer to it as the BLACK TAX CUT, but we have to provide it to ourselves.

CHAPTER 2

The BATTLE

OF THE

THE MIND!

I must say that I am truly proud of my people. Black people are so radiant and beautiful to me both spiritually, mentally, and physically. It is beyond my comprehension how it is possible that we allow ourselves to be as undeveloped economically and psychologically as we are today. We are among the brightest the world has ever seen. It is difficult to imagine how the world could ever suggest that we are inferior or ever could be to any race.

To think that we have such a negative image of one another and that of ourselves is so inconceivable and unnatural and would seem to any intelligent person to be an absolute impossibility. It's like trying to convince a fish that it cannot swim . . . or trying to persuade a bird that somehow flying is too hard. . .it would seem to be a task much like trying to keep the sun from shining its light in the morning or convincing the wind not to blow in the evening. How can a bird not fly? How can the sun not shine? How can the wind not blow? They are genetically programmed and hard wired internally by God to do what they do, and they do it effortlessly.

I realize that the 240 years of slavery that Blacks suffered in this country was an atrocity. That's an understatement, I know. I am aware of the raping of our Grandmothers and torcherings and lynchings of our Grandfathers. It was a brutal time and taxing on the mental state of our generations that is negatively affecting us even to this day. I am by no means insensitive to that. We were chained down like wild animals, auctioned and sold off like horses and mules to the highest bidders – stripped of our human dignity and reduced to mere property.

For hundreds of years we were brainwashed and taught to despise our very existence and hate one another. We were trained to highly esteem White society and a well planned assault was launched to deprogram and eradicate the Hard Drive of our minds. Offensives were waged against anything contrary to the doctrine that we were subservient to and existed only to serve Whites. When I learned that there was actually an organized plan to accomplish this, I was blown away. It infuriated me to think that another human being. . . another race could be so hateful - that a group of people could be so cruel and selfish – that another group of people would have the audacity to oppress and violate other fellow human beings as mere PROPERTY escapes my comprehension.

To think, we were tallied on financial statements and valued like horses, cattle, carts and buggies. Our wives and children were owned by the slave masters and raped and desecrated lawlessly with no shame whatsoever. I cannot imagine wives being taken by the master for the night and made to perform sexual acts to the master's satisfaction and return with shame in the morning to her husband and children, everyone pretending that nothing had happened. That's enough, I submit to you, to cause any rational human being to simply lose his mind.

It wasn't until a couple of years ago that I was privileged to be exposed to information regarding the conspiracy that White slave owners perpetrated against African Americans. It was in a church service during, as best I can remember, a sermon so passionately preached by Bishop David L. White, Jr. of Believers' Victory Center Church during Black History Month. Now I had certainly been aware that Blacks were in slavery for hundreds of years and oppressed by slave masters. I was aware that we were forced to come to this country in the bottom of ships, chained and against our will. I was taught of the underground railroad and Harriet Tubman. While those things were egregious, to learn that experts actually specialized in the science of how to control the mind of the African American Slave just knocked my socks off. I guess you could call the dude an Engineer of Slaveology. And certainly his teachings would be integrated and made a mandatory course in the school's curriculum of that day. Below is a copy of one of his letters:

THE WORDS OF WILLIE LYNCH 1712

"**GENTLEMAN:** I greet you here on the bank of the James River in the year of our Lord, one thousand seven hundred and twelve. First I shall thank you, the Gentlemen of the Colony of Virginia, for bringing me here. I am here to help you solve some of your problems with slaves. Your invitation reached me on my modest plantation in the West Indies where I have experimented with some of the newest and still the oldest methods for control of slaves. Ancient Rome would envy us if my program is implemented. As our boat sailed south on the James River, named for our illustrious King James, whose bible we cherish, I saw enough to know that your program is not unique. While Rome used cords of wood as crosses for standing human bodies along the old highways in great numbers, you are here using the tree and the rope on occasion.

I caught the whiff of a dead slave hanging from a tree a couple of miles back. You are not only losing valuable stock by hangings, you are having uprisings, slaves are running away, your crops are sometimes left in the fields too long for maximum profit, you suffer occasional fires, your animals are killed, gentlemen...you know what your problems are; I do not need to elaborate. I am not here to enumerate your problems, I am here to introduce you to a method of solving them.

In my bag here, ***I have a fool-proof method for controlling your black slaves. I guarantee every one of you that if installed correctly it will control the slaves for at least 300 years.*** My method is simple, any member of your family or any overseer can use it.

I have outlined a number of differences among the slaves, and I take these differences and make them bigger. I use fear, distrust, and envy for control purposes. These methods have worked on my modest plantation in the West Indies, and it will work throughout the South. Take this simple little test of differences and think about them. On the top of my list is "Age", but it is there because it only starts with an "A"; the second is "Color" or shade; there is intelligence, size, sex, size of plantations, attitude of owners, whether the slaves live in the valley, on a hill, East, West, North, South, have fine or coarse hair, or is tall or short. Now that you have a list of differences, I shall give you an outline of action--but before that, I shall assure you that distrust is stronger than trust, and envy is stronger than adulation, respect, or admiration.

The Black Slave, after receiving this indoctrination, shall carry on and will become self refueling and self generating for hundreds of years, maybe thousands.

Don't forget, you must pitch the old Black vs. the young Black male, and the young Black male against the old Black male. ***You must use the dark skinned slaves vs the light skinned slaves***, and the light skinned slaves vs. the dark skinned slaves. You must use the female vs. the male, and the male vs. the female. You must also have your servants and overseers distrust all Blacks, but it is necessary that your slaves trust and depend on us. They must love, respect, and trust only us.

Gentlemen, these kits are your keys to control, use them. Have your wives and children use them. Never miss an opportunity. ***My plan is guaranteed, and the good thing about this plan is that if used intensely for one year, the slaves themselves will remain perpetually distrustful."***

    I am convinced and am going to do my part to make certain that every African American on the face of this planet is made aware of what I call the The Battle To Control The Black Man's Mind. I want to educate every African American regarding these truths not to incite or further hatred or division in the country but to invoke awareness, healing and restoration. Again, many of us in this generation do not know the history of pain, suffering, and mental deprivation that we have endured and thus do not know how to reverse the plague.

Many of us don't even realize that so many of our brothers and sisters suffer from what I have heard referred to as Post Traumatic Slave Disorder. And because we are ignorant of its existence, we do not attempt to treat or counter it thereby leaving it to flourish generation after generation unopposed. I know, mainstream America will attack this characterization once again as another attempt to excuse the behavior of Blacks or to explain why there is nearly 1 Million Blacks in prison today. But please hear me out objectively before you write it off as such.

I have no reservation whatsoever in declaring that Post Traumatic Slave Disorder is a reality in America that negatively affects many African Americans. I intend to prove very clearly this point through very simple illustrations that will not be difficult at all for us to agree upon. First, I know that I have gone out on a limb in the beginning of this chapter remarking how brilliant a people Blacks are- how intelligent, innovative, and resilient we are. I'm not attempting to back up on that. In fact, before I take it back, I'll add more to it! I stand by that portrayal and believe it wholeheartedly. But Goodness Gracious! Do you guys really believe that you can perpetrate he following without any recourse at all?

1. Chain Black people naked in the bottom of ships like animals...
2. Take them to your land to be your slaves...
3. Torture us physically and mentally...
4. Rape our wives, daughters, and sons before our very eyes...
5. Hang us by the thousands upon trees in broad day light day after day, year after year...
6. Auction us and our children off on the auction block like cattle...
7. Assault and Murder us mercilessly...
8. Strip us of every ounce of human dignity and self respect...

All these atrocities African Americans have endured for hundreds of years, generation after generation of being brainwashed and programmed to be solely dependent upon our masters.

Then, all of sudden one day it is declared after a bloody civil war that, "Ok Guys we give up – you can now have your freedom!" Are you For Real? No formal apology, no restitution, no REPARATIONS, and not even a Thank You or at least "We Appreciate" the hundreds of years of FREE LABOR, FREE SEX, and enjoyment of your incredible "Black Woman." You mean we are FREE now with half-white children to raise along with our families which of course reminds us everyday of the rapes and trauma endured on the plantation? We are free with no compensation, no food, no place to live and no bus fare back to Africa. At least America could have footed the bill for a trip back to the homeland. Instead Blacks get a kick up the butt and admonishment to get outta here!

African Americans have endured all of this and someone has the audacity to question whether or not it is possible for some to suffer from Post Traumatic Slavery Disorder? **ARE YOU OUT OF YOUR MIND?** It's a wonder all of us aren't DILIRIOUS! I stand by the fact that Blacks are strong willed and a brilliant species of beings – genius even. But Supermen we are not - immortals we are not. I submit to you that you give us more credit in this regard than we are worthy of.

Still not convinced, let's examine our country's application of Post Traumatic Stress Disorder among soldiers in our armed forces. It is undisputable that our great country readily acknowledges the fact that 1 in 8 of our intelligent and brave men and women (Black and White) who serve honorably in our military are likely to suffer from Post Traumatic Stress Disorder. We have embraced this reality and it is considered a given in this country as we acknowledge the hardships and the devastating psychological damage that can be sustained as a result of war. It bears noting that the average tour of those suffering from PTSD and other related sufferings is 2 to 4 years. If it is possible for soldiers to suffer from PTSD after enduring 4 years in a war zone, certainly one could fathom how 1 in 8 of a race of people who have intentionally been subjected to worse for **HUNDREDS** of years might suffer similarly.

Let me be clear here for the record that it is not my intention or purpose to attempt to justify criminal, psychotic, or immoral behavior by

Blacks. In fact, I believe that each individual bears responsibility for his or her actions and should be held so accountable for the same. I believe that if you do the crime, you should accordingly do the time. I believe also that the punishment should fit the crime and such standard should be applied universally to all. Nevertheless, running the risk of being accused of being a sympathetic, I have to weigh in and respectively declare that African Americans simply got a raw deal in this matter.

One would argue that the PTSD that is sustained by soldiers after being subject a war zone is limited only to those soldiers and does not affect in any way the psychology of their children. That may or may not be the case in those instances. I admit I am not a psychologist. However, when you consider the fact that the entire family unit in the case of enslaved African Americans were subjected to the brutality and mental indoctrination described previously, you could only conclude that the likelihood of this traumatic phenomenon being perpetual is almost absolute. While the soldiers' children were not present and did not witness the terror that their father endured on the battlefield, it is clearly not the case with the Black slave. The wives, daughters, and sons were eye witnesses to the brutality, rapes, hangings, and degradation of their champion – the Black man.

"But that was 145 years ago," some would plead. That's all! Only 145 years? Well, that means we're not even two (2) generations out of slavery yet and considering the fact that the Voter's Rights Act was just passed in 1965, it demonstrates that though Blacks have been

Free for 145 years, we did not realize many of the fundamental rights of Americans until just 43 years ago.

Notwithstanding, we've already managed to get a million Blacks incarcerated in those short 145 years. Come on everybody, there's a bigger problem here than we'd all like to come to grips with. However one might care to characterize it, it can't be justified.

Getting back to the Willie Lynch dude, we clearly see that his plan was genius and it is still working strongly today. Ever wonder why Blacks still refer to one another as Niggers or Niggas, or the "N" Word? Shamefully, we still have not been able to shake this mentally. We have been called Niggers so long that we have embraced the term as a term of endearment but will shoot or cut a White Man who uses it. It is so deeply rooted in our psyche that we have taken ownership of it as our very own. Why would we do that? That's sounds almost insane!! I'm writing this book about the issue and I have to admit that I, too, struggle with the term. That's shameful but it's the truth. This is residue of Post Traumatic Slavery Disorder and the Willie Lynch doctrine still at work.

Mr. Willie encouraged slave masters to pit the light skinned blacks against the darker skinned Blacks. We have shamefully preserved this stupidity over the years and it prevails even today. I remember in grade school and high school all too vividly how the girls only wanted the light skinned brothers and the brothers thought we were doing something when we landed a light skinned girl. It is true to this day. We were programmed to favor the lighter of our race – the closer to White, the better. It is common even now to hear expressions such as, "You're sure getting Black," or "I've gotta get out this sun – I don't need to get any blacker," or simply calling someone "Blackie."

I overheard a conversation between my 9 year old son Zion and my 10 year old daughter Hannah earlier this month regarding this very issue. The bottom line as I remember it was that they had been out in the sun for hours and they were concerned about their complexion getting darker. I was furious but did not miss the opportunity to educate them both on the beauty of their race and attempted to get them to recognize and appreciate their darkness and celebrate it. But who taught them to despise or otherwise seek to avoid darker complexions? I submit to you that it is evidence of residue of the Willie Lynch doctrine and elements of PTSD affecting "even our children," generations later.

Another of Willie Lynch's methods of dividing African Americans is through distrust which can really be summed up as self hate. Mr. Willie was so certain of the effectivity of this technique that he absolutely GUARANTEED that if implemented for just one (1) year religiously, Blacks would be programmed and continue it automatically on our own for hundreds of years. I wish so desperately to challenge his *warranty* as impotent as it appears so simplistic and obvious that a people as great as we are would immediately recognize and circumvent it. Nonetheless what I find is that this technique, though unsophisticated, has proven to be more masterful than them all.

This technique has created what many refer to as the crab mentality among African Americans. Mr. Willie admonished the slave owners to cause Blacks to be distrustful and envious of one another - to under mind each other. Slave masters encouraged Blacks to aspire to reach to greater positions over their peers and showed noticeably more favor to a select few than the others. This caused great division as once the Special Blacks attained those positions of priority, the remaining not so fortunate would envy them and devise plans to dethrone them. And consequently, the Special Blacks (some refer to them as House Niggers or Straw Bosses) would develop a strong allegiance with the Master and forsake unity and brotherhood with his fellow slaves. We were made to strive with one another constantly and would sell each other out at the drop of a hat. We still do this today.

The Slave Masters made it apparent to the slaves that most any one of them could enjoy that position but it could only be earned by undermining other fellow slaves and pledging allegiance only to the Master. It brings my heart great shame to admit it, but this is as true today as it was back then among our people.

Many of us are so critical and envious of our own people that we would much rather spend our money at a non-black owned business and whether we'd admit it or not, subconscious hope that Black businesses fail. Failure of another tends to make one feel better about his own non-accomplishments. The mentality is that if I can't have it, then neither should you whereas it should be if you can do it, then so can I. And I don't have to under mind and seek to destroy what you have to accomplish the same success. This was bred in our race on purpose and we are still suffering from the effects of that indoctrination today.

A good example of this is how Blacks have been programmed subconsciously to patronize White brands in America rather than our own. Many of us do not realize that we wear Ralph Lauren, Levis, and Tommy Hilfiger without giving it a second thought because we've been taught by society that they are the standard. Wait a minute! Phat Farm, Rock a Wear, Sean Jean and many other African American brands far exceed these guys and more accurately reflect our tastes and culture. Yet we would never consider wearing their brands. And I realize that a lot of these brands have been sold off now but my point is that many of us refuse to even consider Black designers because of our negative mindsets.

What's more, in the school systems when our children wear these urban brands, a lot of times they are looked down upon by the teachers. Again, it's okay to wear POLO, IZOD, and others but not anything that a rapper or African American distributes. To them, wearing such clothing brands is negative and counter productive. I ask teachers to be mindful of this mindset and seek to change it as I have to believe they are not doing it spitefully but just out of ignorance, subconsciously.

I submit to you that although it is hundreds of years after the fact, the residue of the Willie Lynch Teaching lives on just as he promised. " **The Black Slave**," he writes, " **After receiving this indoctrination,** shall carry on and will become self refueling and self generating for hundreds years, maybe thousands."

The last and final technique that I would like to expose from the Willie Lynch Letter is that of dependency on the master. Mr. Willie taught the slave owners explicitly to establish an environment where the slave would not think independently but expect that anything he could ever hope to have, could only be made possible by the Master. The slave's natural inclination to Protect, Provide, and Nurture his family was completely stripped from him and the Master became the head of every family unit instead of the Black Man. He had no ability to provide food, shelter, or protection for his family. When an attempt was made to do so, I have learned that slave masters beat the slave to a pulp in front of the family – sometimes would tar and feather them, hang him on a tree, set him on fire and other egregious acts to discourage others from doing the same. I'm no punk but that surely would have discouraged me from trying it.

I have learned further that once the mother discovered how brutal the slave masters were in response to slaves trying to buck the system, she immediately assumed the role of sheltering her precious sons discouraging them from rocking the boat. She began a practice of hiding the young boys behind her in an effort to protect them from physical harm. The father of course was broken by violence and the ultimate threat of death and the boys were taught, though not intentionally, to be wimps and depend on their mammas (women) to fight their battles. If there was a fight to be fought outside with the master, the slave woman would engage the battle while hiding the son inside the house under the assumption that she would fair much better than the husband or sons, especially if she were the least bit attractive.

While this is going on, the father and his sons were cowering in the house as the woman took care of their dirty work. And we wonder why a disproportionate amount of African American men have no shame in fathering children with no sense of responsibility in providing for them. We wonder why many Blacks don't seem to have a problem with welfare checks and section 8 housing being provided by the government – why many of us expect and demand even today that the master take care of us and our families. We were trained extensively in this hundreds of years ago and many of us are still struggling with its ugly effects today.

I have discovered that it was common practice for the Slave Master to require and instruct the strongest Black slaves to impregnate as many women as he could to breed stronger workers. The slave was relinquished of any and all responsibilities in taking care of the babies that he made and a lot of times never bothered to know them. He had no liability at all where the children were concerned. It was understood that the Master would take care of them. And we wonder why our Black males are so indifferent to the four and five babies they make with different baby's mommas, with no sense of obligation to provide for them. We must snap out this absurdity, Black people, both countering and opposing it with everything that is within us. We need to reboot our computers and restore our natural genetics – reclaiming our self-reliance and renewing the pride we once had in ourselves.

We are free now! That was then - this is now! I know and admit that the trauma and the mental effects still abide and are present among us but no longer can we use it as a crutch. Leave White Folks Alone! No matter how many loaves of bread they give us, no matter how many houses they give, no matter how many acres or how many mules or no matter how many checks they write, it will never make up for or correct the virus of STINKING THINKING that we have developed over the years. If we are waiting for White Folks to atone for or somehow HEAL our self esteem, self worth, our family structure, our economic or social condition, we will be waiting till Jesus comes back. While I am not denying their culpability in principle, it is only wise in my opinion to conclude that it would be fruitless to expect them to accomplish for us what can only be accomplished through ourselves.

We must take every opportunity both individually as well as collectively to educate ourselves and challenge each of Mr. Willie's tactics and counter them with the opposite. We must work together to demand an end to our community using the "N" word, through awareness. We need to make a conscious effort to become more trustful of our fellow brothers and sisters. We must make a conscious effort to patronize Black Owned businesses. We must educate our children in the beauty of their Blackness. We must make it fashionable to be of darker complexion. Black men must take our rightful places in the home as protector, provider, and priest. Look around, nobody's stopping us now! We are without excuse!

And finally, we must advertise and expose the Willie Lynch doctrine among our peers and our youth, especially. As long as ignorance of the origin of this stinking thinking remains under cover, its fruits shall survive. When light is shined upon darkness, however, the truth and power of the light annihilates its very existence. I know it seems an impossible endeavor but I am confident it can be achieved. I am certain that once we truly educate ourselves in the root of the destructive thinking we have practiced for so many generations, and apply the counter techniques described previously and throughout this book along with others similar to it, I GUARANTEE that we will REVERSE the effects that the Willie Lynch Doctrine has had on us for all too long.

Much as Willie Lynch admonished his fellow slave masters, I hereby admonish my fellow brethren to apply these principles daily and master them – never miss an opportunity to impose them. Preach these words at the dinner table, from the pulpits, in the school house and in the White House. We must compliment each other when we excel in them and sharply correct those who fall short of and oppose them.

I disagree with Mr. Willie's assertion that distrust is greater than Trust. I disagree with him that envy is stronger that respect. I challenge vigorously his representation that somehow hatred and bigotry is somehow more powerful than love of one's self, race, and country.

Instead I believe that education is far more powerful than ignorance, compassion and forgiveness are clearly more potent than distrust, envy, and strife - and every intelligent person on the face of this planet knows . . .

LOVE is, always has been, and always will be far more superior than hatred and bigotry could ever be.

CHAPTER 3

"LET BY GONES BE BY GONES!"

African Americans have in fact FORGIVEN America for the deplorable acts perpetrated against us in the true spirit of Love. No one can deny it. It is evident simply by the observance of the fact that we live together in harmony and peace and that Blacks have not attempted to kill all the White people out of revenge. While African American extremist are very vocal about the injustices that we as a people sustained at the hand of Whites in this country, I've never heard of any suggesting that we should hang every White for every Black that was hung. I never once heard of a radical Black group of any significant size demand or even recommend that Blacks be recompensed by awarding each Black family unit with atleast one (1) White slave. Although I do believe that the effect of Post Traumatic Slave Disorder is real and that many still do suffer from it, I still believe that the Love of God has allowed BLACKS as a whole to forgive Whites in America for slavery.

I realize that many Whites living in the 21st Century are perfectly content with the argument that they bear no liability for slavery in America as they were not here when it occurred. Many Whites agree that it was shameful and unethical despite the fact that it was lawful. Still, many say, "I have never owned a Negro – I've never hung one – I've never abused a Negro and I've never raped nor have I even mistreated one." For this reason, they assert, it would be characteristically inappropriate to even think of apologizing and therefore giving even less consideration to recompense.

"Wait a minute! I know you are not going where I think you are going with this! NOT REPARATIONS! Just when I was warming up to you and beginning to think you were gonna make some sense of this thing. Now here you come with that Rev. Jesse Jackson and Rev. Al Sharpton, Nation of Islam garbage. What happened to the Peace, Love, and SOOUUL that you were just talking about?"

I know this is not easy for America but I have got to speak truth as I see it. I beg of you, hear me out first. Like Bishop Robert Knight says on the Sunday morning radio broadcast, "Please don't cut me off before you hear the rest of the sermon – Please!" I'm not saying that you will agree with me when I'm done but at least let me explain myself.

I do think America needs to take a hard look at granting some measure of REPARATIONS to Blacks for facilitating the Slave Trade in this country. First of all, let's define the term for clarity so that we may stay on the same page throughout this discussion and keep it in its proper context. Webster's dictionary says it best, I think. They define REPARATIONS as, **1**. A repairing or keeping in repair. **2**. The act of making amends, offering expiation or giving satisfaction for a wrong or injury; something done or given as amends or satisfaction. **3**. The payment of damages: indemnification specifically: compensation in money or materials payable by a defeated nation for damages to or expenditures sustained by another nation as a result of hostilities with the defeated nation – usually in plural.

I think it would be agreeable to all if we summed up reparations as an act of making amends. In America, we advocate both domestically and internationally that civilized people and nations should take responsibility for their actions and when found to be wrong, make recompense. We have taken this position both vocally and in practice for which I am extremely proud of this country. We are a voice in the world for human rights and are usually among the first of all nations in the race to provide humanitarian aid and other relief when we discover injustice.

We rightly require that when companies cause harm to other companies or individuals where loss is sustained that compensation be awarded. When accidents occur whether it is voluntary or involuntary, we generally require compensation to be paid to the victim. Furthermore, it is our long standing custom to require even convicted felons, while they have been given lengthy prisons sentences to serve as a result of their crimes, to pay what we call restitution. Thus, even after serving a 10 or 15 year sentence, monetary recompense is also required.

How is it then that America feels no obligation at all to so much as offer a formal APOLOGY for wrongfully en-slaving African Americans in this country – never mind monetary compensation or REPARATIONS? For this, I say America is WRONG. That does not make me unpatriotic as I am very PATRIOTIC. Being a patriot doesn't mean agreeing with everything one's country does or blindly believing that everything one's country says or does is right. In fact, those who practice that are clearly unpatriotic and their country is doomed to failure if it's full of countrymen of similar philosophy.

I have heard every excuse in the book it seems. However the most formidable one of all is the argument that slavery was legal back then so as a matter of law, there was technically no wrong doing and consequently no justification for restitution, or apology formal or otherwise. Trouble with this argument is the fact that America acknowledges and accepts the benefit of the fact that it was enriched by the hundreds of years of Free Labor at the expense of Blacks, yet refuses to grant a share of the booty to the ones they caused to suffer. And besides that, legality of an issue does not always speak to the morality of the same.

We all are aware that America agreed after years of resistance and fighting in the Civil War to finally grant Blacks freedom. And no one disputes the fact that Blacks suffered tremendously economically as a result of being forced to labor day in and day out without any compensation whatsoever for hundreds of years. Eventually this country was forced to adopt the position that Slavery was wrong and agreed as a result to allow Blacks to go free. They admitted it was wrong ideologically but were unwilling to go so far as to offer a mere apology. Thus they acknowledge that the slave trade has enriched our nation immensely and has made countless White families affluent today as a direct result thereof. Yet, America remains unwilling to: 1. make repair 2. make amends. 3. unwilling at this time to pay damages or offer compensation in the form of money or materials.

Again, White people of the 21st Century owned no slaves and committed no such acts for which they should be held responsible. After all, it was their great grandfathers and great-great grandfathers who reaped the benefits of slavery. White people of today's society did not benefit.

This reasoning would hold true but for the fact that those who rest in this position fail to consider very obvious disparities. While Whites are quick to distance themselves from and accept no liability for the evil acts perpetrated by their kinsmen, they conveniently have no problem embracing and enjoying the spoils that the oppression afforded their generations.

Those same Great-Great Grandfathers left inheritances to 21st Century White Great Grandfathers. Then, the Great Grandfathers of today's Whites left fortunes of silver, gold, farms, houses, and lands that were generated largely as a result of the Free Labor of 21st Century Blacks to White Grandfathers. And many Grandfathers of current Whites have left the spoils to this generation of Whites. And of course Whites of today are enjoying those inheritances. Many of today's Whites are still living in and enjoying some of those beautiful Colonial styled mansions and farms that actual slaves labored to build. Others enjoy their inheritances in the form of cash.

Still not convinced? Some Whites enjoy trust funds and family fortunes that may not be in house or land form which is easier to connect to the slave trade. Nonetheless, I urge you to do some research and begin to trace the origin of the proceeds. It hasn't been that long ago since the Slave Trade was abolished so you won't have to go too far before you find a close ancestor that benefited thereby. Great Grand Dad may have sold the 150 Acres 100 years ago and the family has moved to the stock market since that time, but dig deep and ask a few questions.

- How far would companies like Walmart be in just 20 years if they didn't have to make payroll? You don't even want to do the mathematics. Imagine running your small business today with twenty (20) employees working for free – only allowing them to eat the slops and left-overs from your family's dinner table. Twenty (20) employees' salaries of $15,000 per year equals $300,000 per year. We need not go any further.

The financial benefits of the slave trade are undeniable yet America looks the Negro straight in the face and says, "Hey you're supposed to forgive and forget. Come on - Let By Gones be By Gones!" Bottom line is, the plea bargain America took and maintains is that she will give up the Freedom now and maybe make equality available but as for the SPOILS, that's completely out of the question and Blacks are gonna have to just chalk that up as a loss. You know, sort of like we do in the streets - charge it to the game!

Now I realize that this is largely an unpopular issue to be discussing if one is to be accepted by mainstream America. It is so uncomfortable a topic that even I am uneasy addressing it, I must admit - even as I write. That's another deficiency we have as Blacks - made to feel guilty about speaking the truth to power for fear of being ostracized. What truly puzzles me, however, is that everybody talks about the healing process but what I want to know is how do you truly heal when no one wants to have an honest discussion about what caused the pain, suffering, and loss to begin with. We somehow have resolved that if we pretend that nothing happened, things will work themselves out.

As noble as it may sound, the racial issue in America is not gonna go away by itself. We need to have these discussions. We need to open up and just TALK as a country like we are doing right now. White people need to open up and be granted the liberty to say whatever it is that they want to say however strong it may be – however offensive or not. Geraldine Ferraro tried to do just that and took a beating from the republicans, democrats, Blacks, Whites, and everybody else. This is wrong because we need to have this dialogue. Let her speak! Let me speak! Allow any and everyone who is bold enough to speak to be heard. Lift every voice and sing till earth and heaven ring!

We need to reason together and settle our differences so that we may go on and become the America that we all know we can be. But this can not be accomplished as long as we simply tolerate each other because we have to, instead of making a conscientious effort to settle our differences once and for all. We need to stop ostracizing and penalizing Americans for voicing their objective views, as in the case of Rev. Jeremiah Wright.

I'll go ahead and state it for the record. Though it is down played significantly, Blacks have a problem with two fundamental things concerning Whites in America. Number one (1), White people as a whole and America which represented non-slaves never stepped up to the plate and apologized as a country for slavery. The Civil War ended abruptly without thoughtful discourse about healing and true reconciliation. And Number (2) Blacks in America whether they admit it or not still have a problem with Whites capitalizing all those hundreds of years off the blood, sweat, and tears of our ancestors yet refusing to make restitution. It's more the principal of the matter than anything else even though money does help.

If America had made good on these two issues a long time ago, we'd be a heck of a lot further along than we are today. But it is still not too late. The treasury department is still cutting checks, as I understand it - everyday. And Black people, if I get us this money, you know I get 10% off the top right? Just kidding!

But seriously, there is an estimated 38 Million Blacks in America. I say issue a formal apology delivered orally and in writing by the President and ratified by Congress. Next America needs to cut a check, plain and simple. I suggest take a trillion dollars and settle the score once and for all. Let the economist figure out how to pay for and appropriate it whether it be in the form of Checks, TAX Credit, or other. It just makes no sense that it hasn't been done before now.

Imprison someone wrongfully for 20 years and they're good for an automatic million (and rightfully so) but enslave a whole race of people for a couple hundred years and, "too bad." Maybe it's me but that's just brain-sick. We just granted $700 Billion of taxpayer dollars to bail out Wall Street but we cannot come up with a trillion for Reparations. Give me a break!

I don't mean to rag out the Catholic Church but I am reminded of the complaints of parents of the children who were victims of molestation by priests. Parents complained, as Blacks do about slavery, that while the Catholic Church acknowledges and condemns the atrocities that occurred years ago, they are still unwilling to pony up the monetary restitution that is needed to support the children who were scarred for life thereby. The parents complain that the Catholic Church is not willing to provide the capital that is necessary to render the many years of therapy, counseling, and financial support to these precious children adversely affected. The point is that actions speak louder than words and it is generally much less expensive and taxing to offer rhetoric rather than actual resources. In other words, forgive and forget – Let By Gones Be By Gones!

It's much like two farmers whose 100 acres of farm land are adjacent one to the other. The one farmer is more knowledgeable than his neighbor being a native of the region for over 30 years and his family for centuries. The other farmer inherited his farmland along with 5 new tractors and 1 older tractor from a Great Uncle that suffered a sudden and untimely death. Farmer #2 had never met his Great Uncle. Furthermore, this farmer was very "green" and lived over 2,000 miles away on the other side of the country. He was what we'd call a "country bumkin" just happy to get anything at all. Anyway, Farmer #1 convinced the new guy that he owned only 10 of the 100 acres that were actually left to him and only one tractor. And you know which one that was - that's right, the oldest and most run down tractor of the 6. Farmer #1 assured the other farmer that this was the case and after farming only 2 acres back home and with only a borrowed tractor, Farmer #2 was still ecstatic about his newfound wealth.

Naturally as a result of the use of an additional 90 acres of land and 5 new tractors without cost, Farmer #1 was able to double his profits annually and multiplied his wealth over the next 15 years until he died. His sons took over after that and though they were aware of what their father had done concerning the land, they never disclosed it to their neighbors even though they were friends. Farmer #2 died as well about 5 years after Farmer #1.

It wasn't until nearly 35 years had passed that the grandchildren of Farmer #2 discovered the truth of what Farmer #1 had done. His grand-daughter, who was as honest and pure-hearted as any human being could be disclosed the family secret and the word got out. Now this family had become the greatest of all the families in the region as a result Farmer #1's trickery but (only after years of battle) ultimately were forced to give up use of the land. Nevertheless, due to the great power and influence they had established in the region, they were able to avoid any damages whatsoever beyond simply ceasing and desisting use of the land.

The victimized family was outraged and demanded that justice require the family of Farmer #1 to compensate them monetarily for their loss in addition to awarding them 5 new tractors of the 15 new ones that Farmer #2 had acquired over the years. Farmer #1's family prevailed upon the argument that it was not the grandchildren who had committed the misdeeds and the tractors that the other family sought had already been sold off and were long gone. The 15 new tractors that they did have had nothing to do with the 5 that belonged to the other family 35 years prior.

So there you have it. Take your 90 acres and be happy was the attitude and conclusion of the matter. Farmer #1's family though they put up a formidable defense for retaining the land and ultimately lost it, they were comforted in the fact that they retained millions upon millions in cash as a result that would last them for generations to come. In fact, they gave up farming altogether and went into the banking industry and bought out the major banks in the region. Even then, Farmer #2's family did not receive favorable consideration when forced to take out huge loans with Farmer #1's family bank. After all, business was business – they got their land back, and what did one have to do with the other? "Let's just move on from here and Let By Gones Be By Gones."

I believe America needs to step up to the plate, do the right thing and settle the score once and for all with African Americans. We acknowledge our debt of over $5 trillion to other nations. I just believe America should acknowledge and make good on the debt it owes to Blacks.

It's like trying to be cordial with someone who stole $5,000.00 in cash out of a safe in your home. They've acknowledged the fact that they took it "in so many words" but (number 1) won't apologize and (number 2) won't make any effort at all to pay back the money. In fact, they don't feel any obligation whatsoever to recompense. But they do want to move beyond the hurt, betrayal, and pain in spirit of love and brotherhood. What that person, much like America, is really saying is, "Get Over it Dude! The past is the past! Let By Gones Be By Gones!"

This is the source of the frustration for many African Americans in this country. We can all have overcome and become multi-millionaires but it will still come back to those fundamental two issues. To the man who violated his friend by taking the $5,000.00, be man enough to acknowledge your wrong and offer sincere apology - and for Pete's sake pay the man his dog gone $5,000.00 you took. Right or wrong?

CHAPTER 4

DIAMONDS IN THE ROUGH!

While I believe that America some day will take that noble step toward making amends with African Americans, I am much more concerned about what we as Blacks will do for ourselves in the interim. At the end of the day, the ball is still in our court and it would be superfluous of us to sit around waiting for someone to understand our pain and somehow liberate our race. In fact, the thing that embarrasses me most about our people is our unwillingness for the most part to demand that the giants within us rise up and revolutionize our status in this great country we abide in.

After all it is undisputed that African Americans are notably among the most intellectual and gifted people on face of the earth. Too long have we allowed others to define who we are, who we can become, and the magnitude of our destiny. African Americans have been erroneously taught that we are inferior to the White race and consequently have assumed such roles in our homes, in the workplace, and society in general. Again, our thinking has been wrong concerning ourselves which consequently has produced the distasteful fruits that we have today. A wise man once said, "As a man thinks in his heart regarding himself, so he is or so he will become."

We have been brainwashed with negative depictions and statistics regarding the Black Man continuously and as a result have very low esteem. The residue of the Willie Lynch doctrine still lingers in our environment in this country and it is just the opposite for Whites and their children. White people are over confident and thoughts of inferiority as it relates to their race is obsolete among them. In fact, the very least in the White community often times feel that they are greater than the greatest in the African American community.

This was made so clear to me as I rented some of my nice rental homes to White patrons. I remember reaching out to help a lady who was in a battered women's shelter. Everyone had turned her down with regard to renting her an apartment or house. When I say everyone, I mean all the White landlords because I am among only a handful of Blacks who lease properties as a trade. Anyway, I had compassion on the lady and rented her a very nice property which was completely rehabbed with new HVAC, carpet, paint, and much more.

This White lady talked to me like a dog and dictated to me as if she was my landlord. My strict policy was that tenants could have no pets on the property (for liability purposes) but she demanded after the fact that she could. My strict policy was that she could only have people living in the home that were approved and on the lease. She told me that I didn't know what I was talking about and couldn't tell her what to do so she had at least 6 others. I was amazed and marveled at the fact that this White lady who is fresh out of the homeless shelter (and trailer park before that) was confident enough in herself to speak to me like a peasant.

Keep in mind now, I am a premier landlord with 15 or more properties and she still feels that she is above me. I thought that was fascinating! What if African Americans had that much confidence in who they were? Still, I put her butt out along with the flea infested red cat and the rest of the no-loads she had living with her. But I appreciated the lesson in self confidence. I told my wife, "Now I'm gonna put her in my book!"

Every time we turn on the television it seems we are reminded of how cruel and criminal we are. Rarely do we see positive portrayals and our children feed on these negative characterizations until they become embedded into their psyche. We ultimately get to a point where we come to expect no more than the images we see. We are constantly fed the following:

- There are nearly 1 Million Blacks in Prison
- Nearly 1 in every 4 black men will spend time in prison during their lifetime.
- Blacks are more likely to drop out of school than Whites
- Blacks score significantly less on Tests Than Whites
- Most Blacks have the HIV virus or AIDS

While many of these statistics ring true, they are exploited and overplayed while the sheer brilliance of Blacks in American history is often ignored altogether. I bet you didn't know the following:

1949	Frederick Jones	Invented	Air Conditioner
1892	J.F. Pickering	Invented	Air Ship
1791	Benjamin Banneker	Invented	Almanac
1899	W.H. Richardsopn	Invented	Baby Buggy
1899	L.R. Johnson	Invented	Bicycle Frame
1945	Dr. Charles Drew	Invented	Blood Plasma Bag
1971	Henry T. Sampson	Invented	Cell Phone
1882	Lewis Latimer	Invented	Electric Lampbulb
1867	Alexander Miles	Invented	Elevator
1832	Augustus Jackson	Invented	Ice Cream
1884	Sarah Boone	Invented	Ironing Board
1893	Paul Downing	Invented	Mail Box
1939	Frederick Jones	Invented	Motor
1896	George W. Carter	Discovered	Peanuts
1839	Edmond Berger	Invented	Spark Plug
1876	T.A. Carrington	Invented	Stove

1890	Charles Brooks	Invented	Street Sweeper
1897	T. Elkins	Invented	Toilet
1923	Garrett Morgan	Invented	Traffic Light
1885	Burridge & Marshman	Invented	Typewriter

Imagine where we'd be without these items that we take for granted everyday. And notice the years documented when these inventions were discovered. Notably, most were documented post slavery which one can very conservatively assume that there were many inventions and discoveries of Blacks during the slavery years that we did not of course get credit for. Even still, we've gotta admit that the undisputed documented inventions of Blacks are quite impressive.

Bottom line here is that Blacks have a rich heritage in this country from great inventions to the arts - from sports to politics. African Americans have not been FREE that long and increasingly it is becoming evident that pretty much every field we get involved with (like cream) we rise to the top. We dominate basketball, football, tennis, track and field – you name it. Anything we get interested in and put our minds to, we absolutely dominate it. How can we any longer believe the lie that we are somehow inferior.

It has been said by other ethnicities that we do in fact tend to enjoy advantages in sports where physical strength is demanded but that we lack in those arenas where great intellectual and psychological prowess is key. The great game of golf was their prime example of this theory. Anybody can pick up a pig skinned ball and run while evading opponents a hundred or so yards across a field. But golf, that's a different issue. This pastime can only be mastered by great minds and therefore very popular among doctors, executives, bankers, lawyers, congressmen, and judges. . . you know, those we perceive as he brightest in the world. You know what I mean – White People, Man!

Then comes Tiger Woods, a Black Man, who has absolutely taken over the game and will probably go down in history as the most fascinating and skillful golfer of all time. And on top of that, he was trained from day one by another Black Man – his Father. So here you have the dynamic duo doing great exploits in a highly intellectual sport that has been before now always dominated by Whites.

Now I know, it is highly controversial whether or not Tiger is actually Black especially since White America has embraced him as one of their very own. But Black folks claim him as being Black. I understand that Tiger himself doesn't necessarily claim African American as his race but bottom line is if this were prior to 1860, because of the pigment of his skin, he'd too be in the cotton field beside his brethren notwithstanding any claims of other ethnicities. Now I am no hater by any means. Ask anybody about me. . . they'll tell you, I'm not. But all I'm saying he'd be sitting on the back of the bus like everybody else, eating in Black folks section of the restaurants and drinking from the Blacks Only water fountain like the rest of us. That's all I'm saying - no disrespect to Tiger.

Anyway, the point I'm trying to make is that Black people excel at whatever it is that we endeavor to achieve oftentimes to greater extents than our counterparts. I probably have some White in me, too, but I'm Black. My Momma could have been White or Asian for that matter but I'm a Black Man – Period. The problem is that it's not popular being Black and our children have picked up on it and are governing themselves accordingly. I expect to speak more on this issue later.

Getting back to the issue of Black achievers, we are among the greatest in the world though society has not promoted this image. Instead we have been sold the lies that most Black men are poor, lazy, either on drugs or in prison, unemployed, and absentee fathers. This is untrue but it is bought by our communities much of time as we have failed to celebrate and champion the heroes and positive influences that are all around us.

I am convinced that we have a self esteem problem and it goes back to the conversations on the battle of the mind. Blacks have been told so much that we'd never amount to anything that often times we do not expect anything different. Statistics show that one in 4 African Americans is going to do time in the penitentiary at some point during our lifetimes so we just kinda play out our parts and get it over with. It is expected that many of us will drop out of high school by 10th grade so why not go ahead and get it out of the way. Why wait? And certainly it is expected that Black boys are gonna produce two or three kids out of wedlock some of which while still teenagers so no need to try to get around that. It is inevitable, right?

The problem as I see it is that we as Blacks don't see ourselves for who we really are and thus cannot appreciate our heritage. We have not traditionally seen ourselves as a great people but downtrodden and unfortunate instead. It has not been popular at all to be African American. That's why a lot of times if we can find any loophole whatsoever to disassociate ourselves with our Blackness, we'll leap on the opportunity and take full advantage of it. When our children think of Black, they often think of hardships, sufferings, struggle and racial and social inequality. Many of our youth would love to be able to claim to be mixed -part Asian, part Puerto Rican, part Mexican . . . part anything would help. I know this is another chapter but it goes right back to the Willie Lynch doctrine of self hate and self denial.

We have become ashamed of our heritage only because we are largely ignorant of it. We have not been properly taught the rich legacy of our culture nor the fact that we really enjoy advantages that we have yet to exploit. Instead, we have been conditioned to do everything we can to distance ourselves from our culture and are taught to assimilate and adopt standards that we observe in the White community.

Take golf for instance. You have never seen so many Black Folks out on the golf course trying to become proficient in the sport. Ever wondered why? Well I'll tell you. It's not because Tiger Woods inspired them but more so because for the longest time it has been known as the White guy's pastime. It is fashionable and impressive to Whites to play golf, whether you're any good at it or not. Trouble is, Blacks don't naturally like golf and I'm not saying that we should not but that we just don't. White guys pursue it passionately much like we do basketball and we feel that hey, since they love it then maybe we should too.

In fact, it is no secret anymore that the golf course is typically known as the place where major decisions and deals are made whereas Blacks by default because our disinterest and absence are automatically excluded. So justifiably so, many of us have taken up golf to close this gap and I applaud that. However, a lot of us play the sport to simply fit in and be accepted by Whites and feel better about ourselves.

Again it is dictated to us what we should do and what we should like. I personally have been invited to play golf on a number of occasions by some fat cats and other times been questioned as to why I do not play. My answer is simple. I don't like golf and have no interest in it. I'd probably do very well at it but I simply don't favor it and when I'm asked I JUST SAY NO! Keep in mind now I do realize that I may be missing an opportunity to warm up to a sweet business deal by my unwillingness to pretend like I like the game. However eating cheese has never been my style cause like a colleague of mine so brilliantly stated one time, "Booty Stinks."

If you like golf, then play golf and be the best golfer that golf has ever known. Or if you are bored and want to take up another hobby and are thinking about golf, then hey, go for it Buddy. I'll probably play myself one day. My point is that we as a people need to stop letting society dictate to us what we should do, what we should like, and how we should think. I like what Mohammad Ali said, "I ain't gotta say what you want me to say and I ain't afraid to say what I wanna say." I'm not gonna eat caviar just because you like caviar and I'm not gonna be ashamed to eat my salt mackerel just because you think it's substandard. Hey, I like it if nobody else does. You enjoy your fish eggs and I'll enjoy my fish.

It seems that many Blacks have serious issues with self confidence while in the midst of our White counterparts. This mindset wrongfully suggests that Whites somehow are the standard and that African Americans must adapt to their standards in order to be accepted. We often feel that they must validate a thing before we can fully embrace it. Again, it goes back to the Willie Lynch way of thinking and we must resist it vigorously if we are to effect real change.

Barack Obama is such an inspiration and role model to Blacks because he is so real. This guy is mixed with more ethnicities than you can shake a stick at! Yet he prides himself in being referred to as a Black Man. Wow, what a breath of fresh air! And Barack and Michelle are not the types to try to "play tend" like they are White to fit in. They are a real Black family and I am so very proud of them.

I applaud Hip Hop in a lot of ways to this end. Now please don't misunderstand me. I do not agree with the degradation of women, explicit language as well as the free use of the "N" word. However, Hip Hop is a culture in the Black community where it is clearly demonstrated that those guys don't have a problem being who they are. No matter how much you disagree with them or how much you try to censure them, those guys will not cease to speak their minds and be themselves no matter who disagrees with it. They are not insecure in who they are. They are not trying to be something they are not.

It is not true in the mainstream Black Culture. We are concerned with etiquette and how we are perceived by society. We endeavor to be accepted, seeking approval from the masses and thereby find ourselves not being true to who we really are.

I am fascinated by rappers and hip hop artists even though I am not really into their music at this stage of my life. While certain practices they engage in truly frustrate me at times, I still cannot deny the sense of pride I sometimes get when I see them demonstrate with such confidence unity and resolve in their message. These guys have found a voice for the voiceless and whether the world wants to hear it or not, they have to admit that they find it hard to ignore the power and attention that hip hop demands.

The hip hop and rap artist are largely comprised of our Black youth taking a stand in their own way to advance the cause of African Americans as a whole. Sure, they get bad press because of the cussing, the exploitation of women, and personification of drugs and guns in lyrics and their videos. But wait, we are missing something here. If you really listen, these guys have a better handle on where we should be going than most leaders in the Black church. We are choosing to magnify only the negative impact the culture is having on America and the Black race yet purposely discounting the many positives. We should instead be harvesting the positives (and many they be) and work to redress those areas that are harmful. The good, notwithstanding, far outweighs the bad in my opinion.

But remember, we have been programmed and trained to oppose, condemn, and put down one another. Society jumps on these guys and denounces them with outrage. Then we as a community join in the stone throwing not realizing that in many ways these guys are liberators. Think about it! Blacks don't own any major mainstream networks in America. We couldn't get a message overseas to the masses (or nationally for that matter) if our very lives depended on it. To have any hope of doing so, we would have to beg and plead with mainstream media sources which are not controlled by US, but to no avail.

Hip hop and rap artists can go in the studio, put down their message and ship it out to the world freely on the air ways for the whole world to judge. I think that is remarkable. You mean to tell me that poor Black kids from the projects in south central L.A. can speak to the world through rap and song, and society actually takes note?

I remember so vividly when N.W.A. came out with "f the police" and the song brought such controversy and America was so outraged. Yeah, many Blacks were, too. But many of us were missing the point. What Easy E. and Dr. Dre were trying to get across to the world was what was going in the ghetto as it related oftentimes to the relationship between poor Blacks and the police. Preachers preached about it from the pulpit and congregations of 200 at a time heard it.

Politicians spoke about it at City Hall and a deaf ear was turned to it. Black dignitaries complained about it to each other in the street and you know how much good that did. But here comes what America saw as thugs - "gangs" of Negroes causing trouble by spreading lies and tarnishing the image of police across the nation. But their voices could not be muffled.

You see, these guys created for themselves a national microphone where they could address America and expose to the world what was happening in their world at the time. Yet many of us were quick to ostracize and reduce them to mere street thugs with violent lyrics, as we often do today. But the truth is, Public Enemy managed to accomplish something that many of our Black leaders, pastors, and dignitaries at the time could not. They not only possessed a national podium where they could confront injustices but also made a small fortune in the process. And what's most notable is the fact that they didn't have to sell out in the meantime by compromising their message. Now I, like many others, didn't particularly like or agree with the lyrics but you've gotta admit that they got their point across where we did not.

There are White folks today who still don't get the message that that particular song and others like it was trying to deliver. Take "911 Is a Joke" by the group Public Enemy. Here you have Chuck D and Flava Flav – a pitch black (black is beautiful) dude with an oversized Clock around his neck telling "lies" about 911 being ineffective in his community. These guys erected platforms where they could tell the masses the stories of how different it is in the ghetto. Police didn't always come just because you called them and 911 showed up only after they were sure all was said and done – and sometimes didn't show at all.

This was unimaginable to mainstream America but a reality to poor Blacks in the projects across the country. It is beyond the capacity of many Whites to think that they would be in trouble and in need of assistance from law enforcement or 911 and they not get an immediate response and assistance. Public Enemy exposed these disparities which ultimately led to a dramatic improvement today in those communities that were neglected. But instead of finding the good in these artists, we have been coerced into alienating and persecuting the very ones who have advanced our most precious causes. But remember the techniques of Willie Lynch – he admonished the slave owners to pit us against one another, tear down one another, and most of all be distrustful of each other.

Another point I want to emphasize regarding hip hop artists and rappers is the fact that many of them emerged from the lives of crime in the streets of their communities. Many of these guys were previous drug dealers and gang bangers who if it were not for them pursuing their passion with hip hop and rap would be destined for prison or dead by now. So not only are they giving voice to the communities from which they were ingrained but also many have done great exploits by lifting their families out of the grips of poverty and the suffering that accompanies it. Great numbers have become philanthropists

Bottom line is that many of these guys are just plain genius minds. They have gone from Black kids in the ghetto rapping to becoming major producers and owners of multi-million dollar recording labels. These guys that were once discounted as young Black thugs and dope dealers are major players in the music industry with great influence in our society today.

I have heard stories of how these guys have gone in and completely revolutionized how business is done and deals are made corporately. Keep in mind now these were the so called "low life guys" from the projects standing on the street corner hustling weed and cocaine. A lot of these guys represent the 1 million strong African American brothers doing bids in the penitentiaries across America. They exemplify the fact that our Black youth can do great and mighty things given the opportunity and the right set of circumstances.

These guys are talented artists and everybody knows it whether they wanna admit it or not. Like 50 Cents says, "America's got a thing for this Hip Hop stuff" more so than anyone cares to admit. I'm talking from the presidents to preachers on down to White kids in the suburbs – they can quote the hits verbatim. They denounce hip hop and rap publicly but behind closed door many of them pop in the Tupac Shakur CD when it's time to get it cranking. Preachers will preach against them in the pulpit and discredit their purpose not realizing the power of their influence nor the vast means they have to reach their constituencies. I am convinced that there is a way that we can all come together for good of the common cause we all share. Similarly as the church seeks out the lost and downtrodden and endeavors to lift them up, in many ways so does hip hop in that it offers hope to a hopeless people and inspires them to dream again and offers an avenue to make those dreams reality.

Having been incarcerated myself for 7 years, I have run across tons of guys in the prison system who were brilliant minds. I recall asking many of them individually how such bright guys like them ended up in such a place. And there reply much of the time would be, "the same way you did." The point is this – there is genius in all of us. Some of us have been fortunate enough to make better decisions and maximize our gifts and others for various reasons and as result of a vast range of circumstances chose otherwise. Whatever the choice, or whatever the road we find each other traveling, I think the important thing is to find a way to uplift one another. We must strive to find ways to encourage, exhort, admonish, and aid one another daily in a collective effort to counter the Willie Lynch teachings.

I am convinced that Blacks as a whole really don't know who we are. If you were to ask the average African American on the street some facts about our heritage, we cannot tell you. In fact, if I were a betting man, I'd be willing to take odds that the vast majority of Blacks in free society know less facts about the history of African Americans than those of us who have been or are currently serving sentences in prison. But wait, I'm in no way suggesting that the guys in prison are somehow experts – it's just that I have found when you go down a dead end road and get lost, you are more likely to research where you came from in order to discover where you went wrong.

Still, however, if we gave a pop test on Black History to African American inmates in the penitentiary even 90 percent of them couldn't pass it even if you told them they'd immediately be made free upon doing so. I have to admit personally that I am lacking in this area as well. Even I would have miserably failed if given the get out of jail free opportunity while I was doing time. And more importantly, I'd probably still fail today though I'm currently on a mission to radically transform that ignorance.

What I'm getting at here Folks is that we've been dropped off here on American shores, been enslaved for approximately 265 years, been free for about 150 and that's all we know about us. Many of us didn't know that until we picked up this book. In fact, this book has probably taught us more about us than we've ever known before. And believe me, that's not very much as I am in no wise an authority on Black History or Black Culture. To be perfectly honest, I just learned a lot of statistical facts that I'm sharing this year in an effort to appear half way intelligent about the past while expounding on where we are today as a people. Make no mistake about it, I know full well the predicament we find ourselves in currently but that does not answer the question of WHO we really are.

And no, I am not about to offer in this section a Black History course because as I already admitted, I am truly not qualified to do so. There are scores of Black historians and literary writings available on the market that will begin to fill that void for those of us who may be interested. I have pledged to explore many of them myself and am engaged in their pursuit as I write. But my purpose at this stage is to simply make Black History mandatory for us instead of the insignificant elective that it has been all these years.

I have learned that images are so very vital in the lives of any people and that people will act out on those images and play the roles of the images that are constantly before them. Take the Father of a family who has been a doctor all his adult life and his children grew up viewing such positive images. Ever stopped and wondered why children of doctors very often grew up and became doctors themselves? Ever noticed that nearly all the children of lawyers grow up and become lawyers almost by reflex. The same holds true for the most part with every profession whether it be a banker, congressman, movie star, singer, rapper, or farmer. These images are powerful, I tell you. It's amazing when you truly grasp it. Therefore we can't help but sympathize with the tens of thousands of kids who grow up in the projects with single parents witnessing everything from drug dealing to prostitution on an almost daily basis.

It's fascinating. It seems that images which are set before a people have a sort of power that compels the ones observing to almost effortlessly gravitate toward it. This is true for negative images just as it is with positive. It's harder for a 1st time generation student of medicine to become a doctor than one that grew up around doctors. You see the student that grew up around doctors probably knew personally 5 to 7 doctors of different varieties. This student would benefit from the advantage of having heard the dialogue of doctors for at least two decades before initial study, making him or her a more advanced student by default. This student could probably write prescriptions and diagnose accurately general practitioner level illnesses at a very early age just because they'd witnessed it being done all their lives. This would hold true even if the student really had no interest in the medical field. It's the power of association and the images that have been displayed before them for all those years.

Let's take a typical African American family of 5 which consists of the husband, wife, two boys and a girl. Now for the record, I realize that we have very positive family structures among African Americans (and professional) that are unlike the one I'm describing so don't get offended. Thank God if you are not in this predicament but many Black families are so please allow us to get help. Thanks. Dog!

The Father has worked for the electrical department at the City for the past 9 years and the Mom is employed at the local JcPenney. As you can see this is a very liberal example in which many of the inner city families would consider unrepresentative of their realities. Anyway, the Dad's gross salary is $30,000 and Mom's is $15,000 for a total of $45,000 annually. We can obviously assume that the family owns a $100,000 3 bedroom 1 bath home in a decent lower middle-classed neighborhood. Now again, this is a pretty impressive example but let's point out the images that are before the children.

Unlike the children of the physician, the children of this family are not exposed throughout their childhood to insightful professional images. However, they do have images before them as well that they will likewise naturally gravitate toward. The family and friends of this family many times are likely to be of the same class and status with little variation economically. Thus the children of this class are greatly disadvantaged in that chances are they will simply mirror the images they are exposed to almost automatically.

But the focus here as we move to close the gap of disparities among Blacks is understanding the reality and power that IMAGES have on our children's future. I believe that we have been ignorant of their impact oftentimes and consequently have not made any efforts to improve upon them. The children of this home will not be able to enjoy the natural advantages of those in the home of the physician. The children live in two different worlds which will undoubtedly produce a sharp contrast in their thinking and the grown ups they'll ultimately become.

You see IMAGES whether positive or negative are much better teachers and instructors than we could ever hope to be. Ever wonder why no matter how much the teenage Mom discourages the teenage daughter from getting pregnant and becoming a single parent, the likelihood that the young girl will continue this cycle is almost absolute? Is it surprising that the son that grows up seeing his father verbally and physically abuse his wife will likely grow up and become a wife beater as well despite the fact that he despised his father for doing so? Or ever consider why children whose parents smoke cigarettes or abuse alcohol or drugs tend to emulate these practices themselves though they vowed to never partake in them? What about the fact that children who grow up with the Mom and Dad in the home tend to marry and imitate those very same values.

The old adages often hold true which say," association brings assimilation; birds of a feather flock together; a chip off the old block; apples don't fall far from the tree." We have to learn that IMAGES are vitally important and whether we like it or not they are ultimately going to shape our children's destiny. Good thing is that after being educated in the matter, we can be proactive in the pursuit of transforming those images to effect a desired end opposed to the normal rolling of the dice.

We have to come to understand that the images we see on a regular basis become so embedded into our psyche that they will to a large degree produce fruit that is reflected thereby, almost effortlessly. The time has come that we can no longer afford to just wing it and hope for things to change for the better. Truth is, things will seldom change without someone doing something different to cause that change. Things just don't happen or get better on their own - it takes a lot of conscientious effort and resolve. We have to snap out of this "White folks need to do this or that for us" mode and study concepts and effect mechanisms to make it happen for ourselves.

Images in the lives of people, especially youth, are silent teachers that demand not only that we learn from them, but that we emulate them as well. They subconsciously shape and mold their subjects into the persons that they will ultimately become in life. It is therefore no wonder that children of impoverished homes often under achieve and tend to repeat the cycle of poverty. The same holds true for children who experience or witness disproportionate drug abuse, sexual abuse, and violence in their households. Children who are raised by single parents are subconsciously taught that it is acceptable and perfectly normal, therefore almost assuring duplication.

I guess to sum it all up would be to offer that IMAGES set the BARS in one's life and establishes EXPECTATIONS. We have to admit that as a whole society really doesn't expect very much from African Americans and it starts in our individual households. Certainly we cannot expect the world to expect any more than we expect of ourselves. In fact, we teach others what to expect of us and sadly that has been very little. Strong images in the lives of a people demands greatness and will accept nothing less than what they exemplify. Our job is now to carefully examine these images that are constantly before us and our children – to remove, replace and rearrange as necessary.

Problem with Little Johnny in school is not that he cannot get good grades as much as it is that no one has consistently demanded or expected that he would after he brought home D's a couple of times. After all, Johnny's Dad got D's all through school and barely graduated as well so we cannot expect much more from his son.

And as for La Quita, her Mom was promiscuous and had a baby by age 13 so it's no big deal to learn that her daughter is traveling down the same path and gets pregnant at 15 – then has another child at 17 by a different guy. Hey, that's life.

When boys are uninterested in school, hang out on the corner, hustle drugs in the hood, and abandon babies they have made, it is no big deal or wonder because after all we didn't expect much of them anyhow. And of course with statistics stating that 1 in every 4 Black men will do time in the penitentiary during their lifetime, we're not even disappointed anymore when our sons go to jail because to us like the rest of the world, it is inevitable. Might as well go ahead and get mine out the way early is the attitude a lot of times.

There are plenty of other great things to be expecting of the great minds and talents of our African American sons and daughters. How about expecting thousands of us to fill the voids in the justice system as lawyers and judges in the state and federal systems? What about expecting us to fill seats in abundance in the US Senate and House Of Representatives? How about expecting us to be Presidents, Governors, Mayors, City Councilmen and Legislators?

When is the last time one of us grabbed a troubled youth and explained to him how we are depending on him to be the next great scientist who will develop the cure for AIDS and Cancer which everyone knows plaques our communities and culture? Can you imagine how stunned a young Black kid would be to hear such a mandate being placed upon his life? He'd be like, "Me? Really?" For all he knew, if he just stayed out of trouble and graduated from high school that would be a major upset and he'd be the champion in his family.

However when we begin to show genuine interest and put demands on their lives, we spark the dreamer in our children and their minds begin to posture for the seemingly impossible. I can hear that kid thinking to himself, "Huh, I bet I really could come up with that cure!" But then we would need to get the kid in the company of some real physicians and specialists instead of Uncle Drug Dealer and Cousin Crack Head. This has to be done early on.

We have to raise our expectations and speak them forcefully into the lives of our children until they embrace them. My Dad and Mom spoke so clearly to me that I'd be a successful business man that it formed an image in my mind that could never be erased. I began on a path from that day to this, subliminally traveling toward it. Once the image is formed, it's like a run away train – it's hard to stop. Once that image is formed, without even realizing it you go to work one day at a time bringing to life the picture you have of yourself in that image.

I shared in an earlier chapter how immediately after my Dad began painting these pictures in my mind about age 6, I began wearing three piece suits to school in the first grade. It didn't matter that my friends at the time poked fun at me because of it. My actions began to align with the portrait that was painted on the canvas of my mind. From that day to this, I never did veer off that path of being a business man. In fact, owning my own business is what led to my incarceration. It was just the wrong kind of business and the leaders that were around me at the time including my Father did not DEMAND fiercely enough that I abolish my trade and subscribe to a more suitable. Now many suggestions were made as we often do nowadays, but ultimately I prevailed in my course and paid a dear price as a result. I do not fault my Dad or anyone else because I was old enough and smart enough to have made better decisions than I did.

My point is that we have geniuses among us all over the place and fail everyday to nurture and develop them. We need to seek them out diligently and demand that they contribute significantly to our race, this great country, and the world. We have to declare boldly that they will study hard in school, get straight A's, not ever go to prison, never have babies out of wedlock, and that they will fully fulfill their destiny in life making full productive use of their God given gifts. Oh, how our youth so greatly desire and need to hear these words spoken over them! Oh how they wished that someone would speak such powerful words over them and actually believe in them and hold them accountable!

They'll believe they are great if we will dare to believe it. In fact, deep down within they know it but the negative IMAGES that are stuck on the canvas of their minds overpower the little glimpse of hope that they see through the fog of life every now and then. I am convinced that we will be surprised at what we'd discover if we simply made conscientious efforts to speak to the greatness that is within every soul of our dear children.

We have to stop letting our sons hang out with the drug dealers and the stick up kids in the neighborhoods. It doesn't matter if they are his cousins, brothers, uncles or friends. We must protect and guard against that which is most valuable and that is the IMAGES that are before them. We must articulate to our sons and daughters the demands we have on their lives and get them to buy into them. If they believe they are great, they'll act like it. If we could only paint those portraits to the degree where they are embedded in their hearts and minds, the rest will be history. And when we perceive that our children's actions are not conducive to those images, we must act immediately to defend and preserve our children's destiny, whatever the cost.

CHAPTER 5

BLACK FOLKS

ONLY

SECTION !

*All Non-Blacks are directed to skip this chapter and proceed directly to Chapter 6. Mexicans and Puerto Ricans, O.K.

Alright, let's talk amongst ourselves. I have been eagerly awaiting the opportunity to speak to US in private. By now, it should be pretty evident that I have a pretty good handle on Race Relations in America and that my heart is truly toward effecting positive CHANGE not just for African Americans but also for EVERY American – however, more specifically African Americans. With that being said, I trust that I will be able to speak freely without reservation to those who would characterize my coarse rhetoric as offensive or as "down talking" toward Blacks. This is a grown folks conversation among mature and objective family members so forgive me if I am not condescending to those of us who uphold and pledge allegiance to the Poor Black Victim's Flag.

We have to realize that there are no more excuses. We are among the greatest people the earth has ever known. I'm about to share something that will be life changing to every NEGRO and minority – revelation and good news for all who are otherwise poor, oppressed, or disfranchised. Listen to me good. This is gonna change our lives. Whether we're White, Black, Jew, or Gentile, these powerful veracities will liberate us and will remove the crutch many of us have been leaning on as to why we've got it so bad and cannot get ahead. The truth of the matter is as plain as this.

1. The difference between Poverty and Wealth is Knowledge
2. Whites, Blacks, Jews, Chinese, and German all come from one Race which is the human race. This means there are none created superior to the other.

3. We all are made of the same blood – maybe different blood types but it's all the same blood. Try it – it works in both Blacks and Whites.
4. Everybody has to breathe the same air to live. There's no special White Folks air.
5. Whether you're White, Black, Rich or Poor everybody only has 24 hours in a day to accomplish their tasks. Period. Everybody's got the same 7 days in a week; 30 to 31 days in a month; only 12 months in a year for everybody.
6. The seasons are the same for everybody. It would be unfair if the White folks had summer (or harvest time) year round and we Blacks had to endure the bitter winter for all of 12 months. That's not the case. The seasons are the same for us all.
7. Next, White folks don't get to live longer than Blacks as a general rule. It's all relatively the same duration give or take depending on how you take care of your earth suit.
8. There is no evidence that would positively suggest that Whites possess brains that are more advanced to the Negro which would give them the advantage in excelling more rapidly by default than Blacks.
9. Everybody starts out a BABY! Only dude I know that started out advanced and near grown is Dolemite and we all know he was not real. Even Jesus started out a baby.

I think that if we would spend some quality time meditating on and truly applying the wisdom of the 9 truths highlighted above, we would completely obliterate a lot of negatives that affect our race. The bottom line is that we are ignorant concerning a lot of things. While there are numerous areas that we obviously can significantly improve upon, I am overzealously partial to three (3).

The first issue I want to speak to US about is IGNORANCE. We have got to admit that this is the major of our problem as a whole. I understand that the prevalent connotation of this word is very negative and somewhat degrading to the point that no one wants to be associated with it. However if the truth be told, we are just plain ignorant concerning many things in this country and as a result we are simply getting our butts kicked. And we're gonna keep getting our butts kicked until we wise up and get educated in those areas that we are getting hammered in.

First of all, African Americans at this juncture are not playing on a level playing field with Whites. I realize that everyone will have you to simply forget about race and act like everybody has an equal opportunity in America and that disparities do not exist. That is simply not true. Now I do agree that everyone does have an opportunity but those opportunities are far from being equal. And as I attempted to point out in chapter one, it is imperative that African Americans realize this. Somebody's gotta tell us the truth and I figure it might as well be me.

I know that we have a lot of upper classed Blacks today that oppose this type of doctrine and will swear to you that the world is fair -

that we have realized Dr. Martin Luther King's dream and that racial inequality is no longer a reality. Many advocate this simply because they are now allowed to buy expensive Mercedes Benz automobiles, are able to afford million dollar homes, and can eat in the same fine restaurants and play at the finest White golf courses along with Whites. Granted, things are gravy compared to 50 years ago and I am thankful for the progress, but let's not deceive ourselves into thinking that we're "even steven." This way of thinking while sold to the African American as optimistic can actually prove to be a mis-judgement that leads to catastrophic failure and disappointment both socially and economically.

While I proudly count myself among the chiefest of optimists, I am wise enough to concede that simply ignoring the disparities or wishing them away does not negate the effects that their reality results. It's like a game of spades. You have to play the hand that's dealt to you and more importantly you have to know the strengths and weaknesses of what you have in your hand. You have to keep a watchful eye on the board and know what suit is being led. Just because you have a lot of spades doesn't mean you win every book. If diamonds are led and you've got some diamonds, you're not gonna win that book unless you've got the ranking diamond – doesn't matter how many spades you've got. You'd better watch the board!

All I'm saying here Folks is we have to as a people wake up and begin to operate based upon our keen understanding of the environment in which we live. Everybody wants to believe that the struggle is over but it's obvious that it is not despite what Sean Hannity sells every night on the Fox News broadcast. I hear him over and over attempting to assure America that racism is a thing of the past and that basically anyone who disagrees with that is just out of touch with reality. It sounds so harmonious and every one of us wants to believe him but we, much like he does, know that it is just not true. Maybe he does believe it, but it is just too expensive a lie to subscribe to or for us to purchase at this crucial time. Sean can afford it –African Americans cannot no matter how much money we may have.

The trouble with investing in falsehoods like that is that they tend to give the investor a false sense of security and acceptance that leaves them vulnerable to failure because of it. It is well established and understood in the Black Community that Whites are no better than Blacks. We've known that forever. Go poll the young Black kids in the ghetto about this very issue and 10 out 10 will tell you that. Problem is we have lavished ourselves in the luxury of complacency as a result of this knowledge. Though it is an absolute certainty that we are at the least of par in regard to intellect with our White comrades, that is a major difference from sharing commonality socially and economically.

We have operated under the false assumption that as long as we worked as hard as Whites, were as smart as they are, and can eat in the same restaurants, drive the same cars, use the same bathrooms, go to the same schools, and vote in the same voting booths that we will get the same results as they. Now I agree that we are entitled to the same results but reality teaches us that it just does not work quite that way. We operate as if it does while all the time we are falling further behind and constantly coming up with the short end of the stick. And those who would keep African Americans lodged in this ignorance tend to perpetuate this mindset by crying," RACE CARD! RACE CARD!" every time someone like me challenges it. Keep in mind, though, that every day we remain in bondage to this rhetoric those that sponsor it remain empowered thereby.

There is a saying that what you don't know can't hurt you, but in reality ignorance will not only harm you – it can severely damage, handicap, and ultimately exterminate you given the opportunity. African Americans both old and young walk around every day pretending that the playing field is level when we know dog gone well it is not. Society through news media as well as other venues, have promoted very effectively this disposition and we have subscribed to it hook, line, and sinker, but to our detriment.

The reality, Black people, is that yes we are equal to Whites in regard to everything from our very humanity even down to athletic ability. You name it – physically, mentally, intellectually, socially and academically we are well able to compete - and the list goes on and on. Notwithstanding we do not enjoy equality with them ENVIRONMENTALLY in these UNITED STATES OF AMERICA. This is just fact. Not a put down - doesn't make them better in league nor us worse in class of people. It's just the way it is and the sooner we come to realize this and take corrective action - not by way of the government but by that of ourselves- the better off we will be in America.

Calling our attention back to the nine (9) points offered previously in this chapter but more particularly point number 5, it is in fact certain that we have not exploited the things that are irrevocably common to all. I openly admit that there are many areas where disparities exist everywhere from the criminal justice system to our country's public school system. There are employment disparities, banking disparities, legislative disparities - disparities upon disparities upon disparities. But one thing I am excited about and would like to get everyone else excited about is the list of things that if understood and utilized properly can be employed to neutralize many of the issues that are contrary to us.

I don't care who you are or what color you are – doesn't matter who your Momma is; immaterial is your social status, culture, or even your zodiac sign... everybody only has 24 hours in a day, 7 days in a week, and 12 months in a year with which to deal. Oh, and not to forget that everybody starts out as a BABY!

With that being said, on your mark Black People – get set – GO! Right? Naw, MAAN! See that's my point. We've been running the race like everybody else. We are not like everybody else if we haven't noticed by now. We're Blacks! That's not negative –that's great actually but along with our race accompanies obstacles that put us at a slight disadvantage in life's race that we're running over here in America. It's not terrible news only when we operate cognizant of the revelation of its reality, along of course with the acute awareness of my

Nine (9) Point List as described above. So then it should be, on your mark, get a "Head Start," THEN go!

You see the power is not in the mere fact of just knowing that we all are working in the confines of a 24/7 window but more so the resolve and plan of action of how we are going to use more effectively that time allowance. We have not been operating on a system of URGENCY. It's like we have all the time in the world when we clearly do not. Again, I like using the familiar contrast of the Tortoise and The Hare. The tortoise exploited this revelation better than any example I've heard of in that he capitalized on making better use of something they shared in common, which of course was TIME. The tortoise well recognized his deficiencies as well as the hare's obvious advantages but chose to be the wiser and opposed to subscribing to complaint, he chose to employ the strategy of depreciating the odds against himself by increased hustle.

We all know that the tortoise stood no chance against the rabbit in a head to head match up as rabbits are swifter than turtles by default. Thing is though, rabbits know they have the upper hand so they are vulnerable to neutralization because they are just not gonna work but so hard. They may have 24 hours in a day but "dog" if they're gonna work all of them.

In fact, most Americans are only gonna put in 8 or so hours and that's including the hour lunch, the afternoon nap, and the three 15 minute breaks that most have grown accustomed to. If the tortoise was around in this modern time he'd point out that here is the place we've been missing our opportunity. Moreover he would probably further articulate that the reason we've been missing it is because we have not properly acknowledged the apparent disadvantages we suffer and thus have not purposed to supplement them.

We find this to be true throughout our entire individual lives as well as our generations. From a baby, if we operated under this comprehension, we'd approach our lives and that of our children's much differently. We would labor diligently to set ourselves up for success by out-thinking and out-hustling our counterparts in hopes that when it is all said and done all things would be equal even though the effort was not.

Take the educational system in America – it takes for granted that everybody is on the same playing field from birth to high school – from college to the workforce and business alike. This line of thinking has proven extremely harmful to African Americans as it has promoted an illusion that we have falsely functioned under only to find later in life that it has fallen short of delivering the outcomes it portrayed. As a result, African Americans have blindly followed the paradigm set before us and have heavily relied upon it as assurance that if faithfully pledged toward, we too would attain the American Dream.

Truth is this everybody – we have to remember the tortoise and learn from his example. I understand that in kindergarten it is customary that all the kids take naps for about 2 hours a day to pass the time – that doesn't mean we have to. But it is mandatory, one would argue. My response would be that if we were regular kindergartners, that would be justified but we're not. Just because your fourth grade class takes recess for an hour everyday for exercise, fun, and games doesn't necessarily mean we have to. And if we choose to, doesn't mean we have to do so everyday. Just because the educational system grants all students the benefit of the summer off each year doesn't mean that we have to actually take the whole summer off. Sure, the schools may not be open over the summer but the libraries stay open all year round. Books can be read, textbooks can be studied, vocabulary words and advanced mathematics can be mastered during June, July, and August if only but for an hour a day or just a couple days or so per week. The hare can afford to take the whole summer off but not the turtle.

We all know that the average gig in corporate America is the traditional 9 to 5. Hey, but from what I know about corporate, most executives would be thrilled to allow dedicated workers to stay an hour or so past closing if they feel it would benefit them – especially without additional pay. Being the best is not always good enough because often times we've just gotta be great to be noticed and/or promoted. Many of us are salaried and are under the persuasion that we're not gonna do any more than the next man but still expect to be the chosen one. Get a grip! That may be the case for the hare but for the tortoise that's just not likely to happen in the world that we live. We must operate with this understanding and until further notice govern ourselves accordingly.

Moreover, if we are independent contractors or business owners, understand that we're not gonna get the contract just because we are more qualified and experienced (as we were so certain). We are well aware that it simply does not work that way. It's not even as simple as having the highest quality with the cheapest rate – you'll starve if you believe that's the case. And we've gotta understand that just because we get the contract this year and roll in the dough, we cannot make the mistake of assuming or taking for granted because everybody's happy that we'll have it ongoing. It would behoove us in this scenario to thank God every day and night for things being as well as they are but by all means diversify and work like our lives depend upon us getting other accounts just like it. We have to understand that it is prudent to construct safety nets on various levels at every opportunity to have the very best chance of succeeding. Notice that I did not say it would guarantee our success but significantly increase the odds of it.

Listen Guys, I do not mean to be pessimistic and I am not writing from an angry Black man's perspective. It's just that I expect children, teenagers, young and old adults alike to read this writing and I want to shoot them straight. My goal here is not to make friends. Instead my only purpose is to simply expound upon the realities that we face in hope that our current and future generations will have a better chance when they are up at the bat.

It's okay for Hispanics, Indians, and Jews to educate themselves and promote social and economic empowerment but it just tends to aggravate some groups including "Super Blacks" when African Americans endeavor to do the same. I guess it is so frustrating after witnessing for so many years ourselves as being downtrodden, second class subordinates (to put it kindly) that the very thought of the mass execution of a corrective plan to change that is difficult to fathom.

Unlike us (before now), immigrants who migrate to this great country do not struggle with the fallacies of where they stand in America. Jews especially are fully aware when they come here that the race is not gonna be fair and square. They realize and accept that going in and acknowledge that they are tortoises in a rabbit's land. And of course they are neither bitter nor distracted by it. They take the truths detailed in the 9 Point List and maximize them to the fullest. These guys are truly noteworthy. They own more hotels and gas stations than the White Folks, it would appear. I know that's not the case but they do own a slew of them – that's no joke. Question is, how many do we own?

Unlike us, I have learned that as soon as they arrive in the States, their countrymen who are already settled here formally educate them on the systems of America and teach strategies on how to prevail within. You rarely ever, if ever at all, see them picketing and marching on Washington demanding that America do something for them. Instead they have carefully studied America and while Blacks and everybody else are fighting one another they are employing comprehensive concepts and offenses from within to advance their posterity.

They know they are last in line for jobs and opportunities so instead of crying about not be given them, they just go ahead and create them themselves. They don't have to worry about where their children are gonna work or how they will survive. And they support one another though they may not particularly get along with each other. One thing's for sure, though, and that's the fact that they know that the playing field is not level for them. They know that there are two Jokers in the deck with Deuces wild, and more importantly they know which of them is the tortoise and which is the hare. That explains why when they get to America they land on their feet with their running shoes on cause they know it's gonna be a long hard race.

Hispanics, more particularly Mexicans, are very similar. They know they're the underdogs and don't sweat it. Nobody on the earth works harder or longer than the Mexicans. These guys literally use up the whole 24 hours like the Energizer Bunny. Like my Uncle Bay Bro would say, "I'm not Lying." I know this from experience because I have employed them in the construction industry and these guys' work ethic is second to none. Not only do they work around the clock, they are incredibly reliable and proficient in their respective trades. Blacks, Whites, nor Jews have anything on these guys as they work circles around all of us. And it used to be that they just worked the fields and hard labor jobs that no one else wanted to do. Now, however, they are the contractors and business owners contracting the jobs for significantly less money than Blacks or Whites and in a fraction of the time. Now that's what I'm talking about.

It's kind of hard to discriminate against and black-ball a race of people who bring that type of ingenuity to the workforce. Problem is now all of a sudden America wants to kick them all out the country. I wonder if their rise economically has anything at all to do with it. After all, these Mexican contractors are raking in millions that was once an "all good ole boys enterprise." Dog Gone, if the Mexicans can do it, what's wrong with the Negroes?

You do know that at one time Mexicans were lower classed than us! I haven't seen it yet but we'd better tighten up (Chaps) before we find ourselves riding by construction sites and witness Black Folks working on a Mexican detail. I personally don't think they'd hire us because we probably couldn't keep up with their pace and if they did hire us, we'd be fired by noon because of all those 15 minute breaks we've grown so accustomed to. And I'm gonna tell you now the Mexican boss man ain't buying no chicken for lunch – it's tortillas and beans across the board. Trust me. All I'm saying here is that we would do well to learn these valuable lessons from immigrants who are fresh on the scene in this great country opposed to complaining.

PLEAD THE FIFTH

Okay, enough of that point. Now, I wanted to tuck this conversation safely away in the Black Folk's Section simply because it is vitally important that we as African Americans have the full understanding of this fundamental right. In a time when Blacks disproportionately crowd our state and federal prison systems and that number rapidly increasing, it is imperative that we be educated on the protections afforded to us as provided by the United States Constitution.

Now I am fully aware that many will characterize this section as one that promotes criminal activity and/or educates Blacks on how to get away with committing crime. "Super Blacks" will oppose it, Whites, as well as law enforcement. But watch this – they oppose the education of the Negro regarding this fundamental right that is afforded to all by the Constitution, yet it is printed in black and white for all the world to discover. It is a major part of the highest law of the land in which we live, and goes to the very core of our criminal justice system. Still, it's a problem when it's being taught to Blacks. Whatever!

The Fifth Amendment is thoroughly taught (as it should be) in law schools everywhere and widely recognized and respected by judges, juries, prosecutors, and defense attorneys across the globe. If these guys don't learn anything else in law school, they learn this. Everybody seems to be keenly aware of and therefore employ the power of this amendment when faced with legal problems but Blacks. Even Hispanics when they get in trouble, they know enough about the Constitution to keep their mouths closed until they at least consult with counsel. They'll holler quickly, " No Habla Ingles Senior," when the police arrive on the scene even though they were speaking English rather fluently prior to their arrival.

The Brothers on the other hand, even after being mirandized, will typically begin trying to explain ourselves - "See what had happened was..." This routine course of action has proven catastrophic to African Americans and consequently has made it easier for us to rack up the astounding numbers of Blacks behind bars in this country.

Now I will go ahead and get my disclaimer out the way. The views and opinions depicted in this segment are not necessarily those of the author, his family, or the African Americans in general. Wait a minute – I'm not serious. I'm just always fascinated when I hear that on television and radio broadcasts before or after controversial messages and always wanted to use it myself. It really doesn't apply here because these views and opinions quite accurately reflect my views and I stand by them wholeheartedly. But understand that I am speaking for myself here.

I will add in advance, however, that I strongly advise everyone reading this chapter to simply abide by the laws of the land where hopefully these teachings will not need to be employed. I always say anyhow that Black Folks can't afford to get in trouble to start with. There's trouble enough being Black alone without adding the foolishness of criminal conduct to the equation. In fact, we were born in trouble.

Furthermore I believe that if one so chooses to practice criminal behavior then the penalty that awaits should be his or her fate. There's my true take on the issue of criminals for the record so those who would quote me, please be sure to do it accurately. If it were anything other than that, I wouldn't be afraid to tell you. Again quoting the great Mohammad Ali, "I ain't gotta say what you want me to say and I ain't afraid to say what I wanna say."

Please allow me to go ahead and quote the Fifth Amendment as adopted by the US Constitution instead of assuming that all have read it. It reads:

'No person shall be held to answer for a capital, or otherwise infamous crime, unless on a presentment or indictment of a Grand Jury, except in cases arising in the land or naval forces, or in the Militia, when in actual service in time of War or public danger; nor shall any person be subject for the same offence to be twice put in jeopardy of life or limb, **NOR SHALL BE COMPELLED IN ANY CRIMINAL CASE TO BE A WITNESS AGAINST HIMSELF,** nor be deprived of life, liberty, or property, without due process of law; nor shall private property be taken for public use without just compensation.'

Okay, while there are many jewels of protection that can be found in that great passage, I endeavor to expound upon only one. I'm very serious about this issue and it could very well be the most important thing that a person will read in this book. This chapter and maybe even this very segment right here will actually save a lot of Negroes' lives if we will heed to it. This teaching should be mandatory in the curriculum of all African Americans in every part of the country – doesn't matter if we're upper-classed, middle-classed, lower-classed or have no class. If one is Black living in America he or she (that's right she, too) needs to fully comprehend the significance of truly understanding and applying the Fifth Amendment.

You know it's funny how I tend to get an uneasy feeling when speaking about this issue because of the critics and what is sure to be their negative portrayal of this doctrine. But at the same time - it seems- I also enjoy the sense of pride in knowing that this dialogue is monumental in the fight to educate and empower our race to succeed in these difficult times. I might add also (at the expense of being further isolated) that while they will crucify me for freely teaching it to African Americans, they will not openly admit that it is a subject that is privately taught among themselves. Their children are scholars in these principles which account for a lot of the disproportionateness we find in why the percentage of Whites charged with crimes receive significantly less time and/or convictions than those of Blacks.

How hypocritical is that? Prosecutors, judges, congressmen, lawyers, and law enforcement officials will openly condemn the teaching in this context to Blacks but I bet every single one of their children know well how to conduct themselves should they find themselves faced in criminal inquiry. That goes for Blacks and Whites in those professions and I agree that they should teach their children as much. All I'm saying is don't knock the little guy who wasn't fortunate enough to attend an ivy league law school but still wants his family to enjoy full access to the antidote. I mean, give a dog a bone here Folks.

Anyway, the Fifth Amendment (the portion we are to discuss) provides in a nutshell that we have the right to NOT be forced to testify or be a witness against ourselves in any criminal case or investigation. Now it is trivial as exactly when to invoke this right because often times it can be kind of difficult to determine when we are actually the subject of a criminal investigation. I know this may sound kind of base to many but a lot of times the simple truth is that being Black in America, we are almost always ATLEAST the potential subject (or suspect) of an investigation when questioned by law enforcement. I'll say it again for clarity. As African Americans, we are almost always suspect when we are subjected to questioning by persons in authority whether it is represented as such or not. Like the preacher often says, "I'm preach'n a whole lot better than ya'll are saying Amen!" You know I'm right. We have been confused as to when we are actually being investigated or suspected. Blacks are suspects or suspicious almost by default.

I can hear Sean Hannity saying, "That's just a bunch a crap – 90 percent of White people today including those in law enforcement do not share such a preposterous view." If that's true then please explain to me why Blacks are still profiled disproportionately from shoplifting when in expensive stores to being "out of place" in a nice neighborhood, all the way down to just driving along in a luxury automobile? Tell me why it is still common to have White women (not all, we know that – calm down) clutch their purses while in elevators among even professional Black men? And explain why still today if there is a robbery or shooting police tend to seek out the nearest Black guy in the vicinity for interrogation? Keep in mind at this point they are not considered actual "suspects." That doesn't officially happen until their answers to the questioning of investigators are unsatisfactory and the subjects have already incriminated themselves.

We have to come to understand that no matter whether we think it's fair or not, just or unjust - bottom line is that it is reality. Just like in the case of Hispanics, police wrongly profile them in assuming that pretty much every Mexican is without a valid driver's license – or worse, if they do possess a driver's license, chances are it's a fake. Do you know how many Rodriquezs, Carlos, and Garcias there are in America? Nearly all Mexicans are one of the three about like 9 out of every 10 Indians are Patels. Am I right? Come on now, many of you agreed but that is just not accurate. Nonetheless, you get my point about perception and stereotypes.

I, for one am happy to know that while I may be profiled as a petty thief, bank robber, murderer, pimp, or drug dealer, at least I can take comfort in the fact that it's highly unlikely that I'd be suspected of being an illegal immigrant or terrorist in America. After all, the White folks can't get away with that one because they're the ones that brought us here! At least it is assumed that Blacks will, for the most part, have a valid driver's license at such time as we are unfairly targeted by troopers and police in a traffic stop. And while we will get the occasional frisk at the airport checkout more than we feel is merited, at least we don't have to go in the security room every single time like the Indians and the Arabs. It's pretty much a given that Negros aren't hijacking any aircraft. We do get the benefit of the doubt in these regards I must admit - and for that, we give thanks.

Getting back to the Fifth Amendment, we don't use it nearly as much as we should and it is truly shameful that we have not taught our youth its significance. I realize that our focus should rightly be on teaching them right from wrong and encouraging them to steer clear from every appearance of trouble, but I think this needs to be taught as well – not to facilitate negativity but instead as a buffer in the unlikely event that they find themselves in trouble. We error in falsely assuming that if we ignore the realities of these types of things occurring, it will somehow make them less likely to result. The nearly 1 million of our sons in the prison system is proof that this way of thinking is ineffective.

The Fifth Amendment asserts that we have the right to not be compelled to testify against or incriminate ourselves. Or to put it quite plainly, we have the right to remain silent or shut up when it comes to telling on ourselves or helping the police or others in authority build a criminal case against us. Now we have talked a little about these rights only being applicable in the instances where there is a criminal investigation or one that could potentially be criminal. We have found that the problem with this posture is the fact that authorities in law enforcement have become very clever in their tactics with regard to informing suspects of their intent when questioning.

For example, let's assume there was a shooting that just took place only 10 minutes earlier at a night club and a Black 19 year old was pulled over by police shortly after, as it was told that the shooter had fled the scene. Now nobody so far appears to have gotten a good look at the shooter because of course it was so dark in the club and everything happened so fast. All the witnesses however could attest to the fact that the shooter was a Black guy -young between the ages of 19 and 25, 180 pounds or so. It just so happened that the night club in question was only 3 blocks away from where the young man is stopped. Two police cars are on the scene and they radioed for the lead detective to come down and assist in the questioning. The detective pulls up and approaches the young man who is still patiently seated and waiting in his automobile. The detective calmly asks for the young man's license and registration – no weapons pulled or any sign that this is anything other than a routine traffic stop. The detective doesn't get excited at all and even addresses the young man as Mr. So and So before he proceeds to ask the magic question. "Where are you coming from?" Now Friends, what this young man does at this point could mean life or death for him, or at the very least determine whether or not he spends the night at home in his own bed or in the county jail.

Now watch it. This guy, if he knew what the context of the questioning was, and having been educated in and following the protocol outlined in this segment, would not tell that detective that he was anywhere near that club – whether he was or not. I can hear the critics raving at this point that what I am suggesting is totally outrageous. Wait a minute give me a chance to finish my workbook exercise. Regardless of whether the young man was at the club or not, my suggestion is to simply provide the detective with his license and registration and make the following statement. "I admit no wrongdoing and decline to answer any further questions and respectfully request that I be allowed to be on my way." If the detective persists with further questioning, it would be advisable for the young man to repeat his previous statement and add the following: "At this time I'd like to assert my Fifth Amendment privilege afforded by the United States Constitution." Further if the young man is under 18 or still lives with his parents, he should immediately request that his parents be telephoned but under no circumstances should he proceed with the interrogation (which is not at this point considered such).

You see what often-times happens in situations like this, especially when there is no clear eye-witness, pressure begins to rise on everyone to draw conclusions. If this guy says he was at the club, chances are he's in for a very long night whether he had anything at all to do with the shooting or not. Once he admits to being there, he has just heightened his chances of being arrested and set himself up to be the prime suspect which directs everyone's focus and attention on him. Whether he's the guy or not, when he admits he'd just left the club, detectives began to feel a sense of relief as it is likely they've got their guy or at least someone who can provide information on their guy. This guy's answer of yes to this question effectively incriminates the fellow because his own testimony places him at the scene.

First thing they'll do under these circumstances is to ask if he would be willing to clear his name as to a shooting that occurred back at the club because they are sure he wasn't the one who did it. The detective offers that he is sure that it'll only take a few minutes and asks very cordially if the young man would ride with him back down to the club to clear everything up – in his unmarked and un-caged cruiser of course. Naturally at this juncture, the young man feels compelled to go especially since the authorities are treating him so well and appear to believe he is innocent of any wrong doing – all this is more so to eliminate him as a suspect altogether. Whether he was the shooter or not, no one would be able to positively I.D. him so agreeing to go couldn't be a bad idea either way.

Problem is this. Whenever a detective along with two or three other police cars pull back up to the scene of any crime with a Black man in the back seat (marked or unmarked police car), it is assumed that they have found their guy. All someone has to do is positively I.D. him.

Doesn't matter if he's brought to a White crowd, Black, or even Hispanic – the assumption is that they must have found the perpetrator. Naturally someone's loved one or friend is hurt or even dead so the bystanders are distraught at this stage and eager to hold the one who did it responsible. Many times before the officers can even ask, "Is this the guy who did the shooting," witnesses are already pointing and actually ready to jump on the guy out revenge before he even gets out of the cruiser and they get to see his face. Remember now it was dark, disco lights flashing, and commotion all over the place so it would almost be impossible to positively identify anybody as the actual gunman in this case.

Rumors had circulated among witnesses that the shooter was seen fleeing the nightclub and here is a guy seemingly caught by police just a short time later. What are the witnesses supposed to say? "I'm not sure if this is the guy or not – it looks like it could have been but I can't say for sure." Do you really expect these witnesses to be that objective under those difficult circumstances of fear, sorrow, and anger running so very high? Do you really expect them to give a free pass to the potential killer and let the one who might have severely injured or killed their loved one or friend go free? Just like that? Don't hold your breath. What is more likely to happen and this is just giving the dude the benefit of the doubt, is that witnesses will offer, "I can't be 100% sure but I THINK that's the joker."

The young man at this point begins to panic and proceeds to act like a criminal in his attempt to defend himself against the "alleged" false accusations. He begins to get loud and irate out of desperation and at this point appears to officers and others as a possible threat. Now bear in mind that up to this point he was not in any hand cuffs but the officers feel compelled at this juncture to at least handcuff him if for none other's, his own protection. More questions begin to be fired at the young man and if there were any doubt whether he was a suspect before, it is quite evident that he is at this stage. Only now the young man is desperate to convince them somehow that they have got the wrong guy and that the witnesses are mistaken. He therefore resorts to the unwise choice of fabricating a story in a failing attempt to prove his innocence. The story meanwhile doesn't check out and actually conflicts with statements that the suspect made earlier when he was supposedly not a suspect. To make a long story "shawt," the young brother is in a boat load of trouble and in for a long night.

It is at this point that the poor teenager realizes the fact that he is in need of some serious help. After calming down he requests that his parents be called as he is being taken down to the precinct. His car just down the street is being searched in the mean time for the gun and other related evidence. When no gun is found, the vehicle is towed to the police station for further forensic examination. The club is shut down and the crowd disperses as they witness the young man being taken away in the caged police cruiser. The crowd disperses. "I'm glad they got em," one witness says. What's more, as the patrons of the club are leaving, one after the other sees the scene down the street where police cars have surrounded the young man's car and are proceeding to have it impounded.

Well, I'm not gonna prolong the story neither will I disclose whether or not the fellow in custody was the right guy or not because that's really not the point. The point I'm trying make here is that whether we're guilty or not, the best course of action to take when confronted is to exercise the Fifth Amendment privilege granted by the constitution of the United States Of America. Critics will argue that if you did it just fess up, take responsibility, and do the right thing and trust that the prosecutors and judges are gonna be fair to you in punishment. I truly wish it were that simple for Blacks but we all know by the statistics that it is clearly not the case. I do agree that perpetrators of crime should take responsibility and be contrite but exposing one's self openly to the courts as such is something I oppose vehemently.

Whether guilty or innocent following the protocol outlined in this segment can ultimately mean the difference between life and death. If the subject was innocent, he could have spared himself and his parents a whole lot of heartache, sorrow, and bond money as well as attorney's fees if he'd just offered the police my "statement" when pulled over. If the officers persisted and arrested him, they would have at that point read him his Miranda rights which would have been the clue to take them up on the offer by remaining silent. Upon being arrested he would not have been taken before the impatient and desperate crowd at the night club but to the police station. His parents would have been called and hopefully an attorney. Witnesses would have been brought to the police station where a proper line up for identification would have been performed. Long story "shawt," this young man would have been on his way with no bond, no witness I.D., and no evidence whatsoever of any wrongdoing as there was none.

Take the other scenario where the young man was the shooter and was in fact guilty and the victim died. The young man invokes the fifth amendment, goes to the precinct and calls his parents and just any decent traffic court attorney. He's subjected to a proper line up and witnesses come in and of course are unable to positively identify him because as we recall it was just too dark in the night club. The murder weapon was not found in the automobile and because there is no further evidence linking the suspect to crime, he too is released in the custody of his parents with no bond.

However because this is a really good kid from a great family who simply got caught up in a terrible situation where he panicked and made a stupid decision, he with the counsel of his Mom and Dad decided to take responsibility for what he'd done. They did this with the benefit of the advice of competent counsel outside of the jail house and were able to strike a fair deal with the prosecutor. Instead of a life sentence or 40 years or so, he was able to plead to manslaughter and received a sentence of 15-20 years. The prosecutor had no other choice but to agree because without the young man's testimony, it would have been doubtful that any charges at all could have been sustained. This scenario could have only been made possible by the preparation and application of the protocol as recommended in the segment. Otherwise, even in the event that it was proven by prosecutors that he was remorseful and fully cooperative, the chances that he'd see under 35 years would be slim to none. So in any case, asserting his Fifth Amendment privilege would have naturally been in his best interest.

It is commonly known that among serious criminal defense attorneys that when initially pleading at arraignment hearings as well as at booking, that defendants are almost always advised to plead NOT GUILTY. They can be as guilty as sin and actually caught red-handed but the general consensus is to take the fifth and enter a plea of not guilty. What this does is gives the appearance that the defendant is up for a fight though the odds are most certainly against him and puts prosecution on notice that unless they are willing to offer concessions of some kind, that they will have to work for every minute of their procurement. Pleading guilty and offering further incriminating statements on the other hand merely serves to discourage incentives offered on the part of the state and closes doors to negotiations. After all, in order for one to negotiate, he has to have something to offer that is not already freely available.

I realize this must sound disgusting to many especially Super Blacks who would simply say that Black people just need to stay out of trouble. And I agree wholeheartedly with that counsel, but the question is what's your advice to troubled youth who find themselves therein, notwithstanding? Just throw em all away? Trouble with that way of thinking is that once many of our youth get their thinking straightened out and are committed to making a positive contribution to society instead of being a detriment, they've been stacked up with so much TIME (40 to 50 years) that it's darn near too late or they're too old and mentally stifled to offer very much. Often times they don't get a second chance after receiving a 40 years to life for a crime that their counterparts only received 10 to 20 years for every day of the week. Sure, abstinence from crime is the key and I promote it constantly but education in this context is equally as significant given our prognosis.

My primary concern is that of our children. During my years of incarceration, I sadly came across scores of young Black men with prison sentences that were simply mind boggling when matched with the crimes that had been committed. And over and over I found that in most cases the common denominator was the fact that the inmates themselves were the chief witnesses against themselves. While clearly none should by any means have expected to have gotten away with any of the crimes committed (me included), certainly they would have received in many cases only a fraction of their sentences if they had defaulted to protocol.

Let's not kid ourselves though, exercising the Fifth Amendment should be taught to our children much earlier than the ages where our children are old enough to get into situations where incarceration would be the penalty. I advocate that this is something that should be taught and universally practiced at grade school level as well. Ever been to the principal's office for misbehaving or "cutting shine" as my Grandma Celian would call it? How many times have you encountered the teaching staff or principal interrogating students to get to the bottom of a serious school incident? What? You guys have never done anything wrong have you? I'm not mocking because I wish it were me instead with that testimony. It would be someone else writing this book while

I'm this big time Corporate Attorney representing Fortune 500 companies.

For the benefit of the "goodie two shoes" (which I envy), here is how it goes down. Say a 9 year old fourth grader squeezes a little girl's backside in the hallway as was quite common back when I was in school. And I mean he gets a good hand full and of course the girl tells her 4th grade teacher that she believes he is the one who did it. The teacher follows school policy and notifies the principal. Therefore off goes the little boy to the principal's office which is just short of an interrogation, under these circumstances anyway. I can never remember going to the principal's office for any reason other than the result of my misbehavior of some capacity and the purpose for the visit was always interrogation-followed by punishment. Again, my position is that every Black boy or girl should simply do as they're told, act right, and stay out of trouble to start with. This is not designed as a tool to aid and abet disruptive and unlawful behavior.

Moving right along! The principal is going to conduct his or her investigation to ascertain the facts of what transpired. Much like that of criminal investigators (or parents) they will employ every tactic available to induce a confession from the alleged perpetrator. The 9 year old 4th grader doesn't stand a chance under such examination and many of you would say that he shouldn't – and maybe you're right. Nevertheless considering that the fourth grader could actually be expelled because of the act or possibly summoned to juvenile court regarding it, I would offer that at the very least the boy's parents should have been afforded the opportunity to be present at the deposition. But naturally it isn't until after the confession and the suspension and all the pertinent decisions have been made are the parents called, which at that point it's a done deal.

The boy just forfeited that school year and repeats the forth grade all over again. And keep in mind the girl testified that she couldn't be 100% sure that he was the one who did it as the hallway was crowded. She assumed it was him because he had a stupid grin on his face that she wanted to punch off when she immediately turned around. Now we all know the boy did it but no one else claimed to have seen him do it including the victim.

Now in this case we can all agree that while the boy was absolutely positively dead wrong, like in most cases a firm rebuke and couple of good licks on his backside by the principal as well as his parents would have more than likely done the trick. And the punch in the mouth that the little girl was thinking wouldn't have hurt either. After all, the boy was a decent kid and was actually very disappointed in his poor choices and was genuinely remorseful. I know this must sound appalling to many but we simply cannot afford to take for granted and blindly rely upon the administration of justice by others at this time. If he had only been taught to exercise his Fifth Amendment privilege and allow his parents to deal with issues regarding authorities, he would have been spared the severe penalty of expulsion while at the same time proving worthy of the grace by never repeating the act or misbehaving as such again, as a result.

The preventative answer, of course is for everybody to just do right and simply stay out trouble but as we are aware, that's simply not going to be the case for all. There are just gonna be times where some of our children mess up. It is important during such times that while we ought to make sure that they are disciplined effectively, we must also ensure that they are not disproportionately impaired during the process.

I'll never forget two best friends – there names escape me- who were only 15 and 16 years old back when I was at what's known as High Rise Youth Institution in Morganton, North Carolina. The official name is Western Youth Institution but on state it's only referred to as "High Rise." These best friends that I made mention of accompanied me on the 14th floor of the building in which all of the Close Custody inmates were held. If you were on the 14th floor back then, you were classified by the system as an escape risk and generally had a sentence of 25 years or more. I remember my wife, who wasn't my wife back then, and Mom coming to visit me during that time and trying to make out who they were through the day room window. However, we were so high in the sky that it was literally impossible. Despite my perfect vision, everyone on the ground appeared as ants and it seemed that freedom was as far away as they all appeared. Forgive me if while telling this story I tend to drift off in retrospect as I find myself doing right now.

Anyway, as I got to know these two best friends I was deeply moved with sorrow as I learned how well-mannered and big hearted these kids were. I refer to them as kids despite the fact that they were only two years beneath me at the time because they behaved like your ordinary 8th and 9th grade students. They were annoyingly carefree and playful and behaved more as if they were away at boys scout camp instead of the penitentiary. I recall them addressing the correctional officers as yes and no sir and it was evident that these guys came from loving homes where they were taught to respect their elders. It didn't seem to dawn on them that it wasn't a particularly good idea for them to appear so soft spoken in such a place that demanded more malignity.

As it turned out, I later learned that these two fellows had received sentences of 100 years (for the younger) and 90 years (for the elder). They were nicknamed Hundred Bones and Ninety Bones by the other inmates referring to the amount of time they caught. One of them explained to me how they were out goofing off in the country one evening playing with a loaded gun they'd come across. A state trooper happened to come by and stopped to question them. The 15 year old panicked and shot the trooper in head killing him on the spot. I guess that explained why he got the 100 bones and I assumed his friend got the lesser because he didn't pull the trigger.

I didn't even want to hear the rest of the story. How easy it is to literally throw the rest of your entire life away in an instant and likewise destroy many others. I am sympathetic to the trooper and his family as well as the two young boys and theirs. That was 1991 when I met them so they have to be about 32 and 33 years old about now with 73 and 83 years to go minus good time. Stories like these as well as mine are all too common among our race. My hopes are that somehow, someway I can make a difference through education and books like this one that would effectively save troopers' lives like the one that was lost, spare his family the grief and loss, and foster better decisions among youths who would falter so miserably as these two.

I must admit that it is so very difficult to write advising people to exercise these rights while knowing that many will opt to abuse the information thus making it more difficult for law enforcement, and in some cases crimes will go unsolved. Believe me, the very thought of such is quite disturbing to me as I'm sure it was for the patriarchs who ratified the protections. But as they were strong in their convictions, I must likewise be. My prayer is that the abusers will reap the reward in full measure of their seed planted. But my purpose is that African Americans ignorant and therefore destitute of the power and mercifulness of such a privilege also be the beneficiaries thereof, in spite of them not having attended Harvard or Yale.

And before I move on, let me just say this. Whatever you do, please exercise this option whenever dealing with federal authorities about even the smallest issue. Never lie to them as that is their favorite charge. They will be investigating you or someone else about a real crime and cross you up in a lie and charge you with the lie. They will do this while completely forsaking the charge that they were initially pursuing. Craziest thing I ever heard of. They'd rather have that charge than the original. Black people are ignorant of this until they find themselves caught up in it. FYI.

Parents teach the kids to stay out of trouble. However while doing so, please do not fail to teach them to always exercise the fifth should they find themselves therein. Make sure that they know to shut up and call you in the untimely event something like this should happen. This goes for school or otherwise. Many times kids figure they can talk themselves out of the trouble in an attempt to keep from getting in trouble at home with you. In the process, they dig themselves deeper but it's because they have not been properly educated by their parents. We as parents are home with our fingers and toes crossed merely a hopin and a wishin and a prayin that nothing happens. Look where that has gotten us! Hope is not a strategy - education is the key!

AIDS IN THE AFRICAN AMERICAN COMMUNITY

It is astounding to me and should be to you as well the recent statistics revealed about Aids in America. Recent reports show that over 1 million people in the United States either have AIDS or are HIV Positive with over half of those affected being Black. It is disturbing to learn that anyone has to suffer with such a dreaded disease in this country but even more appalling is the fact that Blacks suffer so disproportionately. While we comprise only about 13% of the population, we represent as much as 60 percent of the aids cases. What's more, it is reported that as many as 1/3 of all people infected don't even know that they are infected with the disease and continue to spread it.

The problem is that everybody it seems is afraid to get tested so not very many people know their true status. It is a fact that by the time most couples are married that they have had sexual intercourse with at least 3 to 5 different partners and for those who do not marry which are approximately half engage in intercourse with at least 7 to 9 different partners over a lifetime. Mind you these are figures for ordinary Americans that have what many refer to as normal sexual behavior not rising to the level of promiscuous. Therefore with the numbers being as such, it's no wonder the statistics are the way they are. I also believe that one of things we need to focus on is quality health insurance and competent health care providers in our communities.

Bottom line, Black people, is we are not dealing with this issue intellectually. The statistics are real – we cannot ignore them. Every African American who is sexually active whether we are married or not (that's right) needs to get tested immediately. That means NOW! And everyone of us that gets tested should make certain that everybody else that we know gets tested as well. It could very well save ours lives and those of our loved ones. And later for that cop out that would suggest that we know we don't have it. We don't know a dog gone thing until we get tested and confirm it. We believe and hope to God Almighty we don't have it but we have to KNOW. Ignoring the possibility or simply hoping we don't have it doesn't make us not have it. Nor does it treat or cure us if we do have it. And it certainly does not stop us from spreading it in the event that we are in fact infected.

It is absolutely ignorant of anyone sexually active, especially Black people, given the alarming statistics to have sex with someone without both parties first getting tested. Just because we are not sick or have the symptoms of AIDS victims as of yet doesn't mean we do not have the disease. Ask AIDS patients and they will tell us that they didn't have any symptoms or signs either until they all of a sudden started having symptoms and signs. DUH! And of course every one of them thought just as all of us that it could not happen to them – that the partners they slept with did not look like they had AIDS. Trouble is that if AIDS had a look or a certain face, we'd all have avoided it and none of us would have the dreadful disease. And furthermore, I wouldn't be writing about the epidemic in this segment.

So what that we're settled down now and happily married enjoying a faithful relationship without any outside vulnerability. The danger is that we can't be sure that the outside dangers are not already inside because one or both partners brought it in when they came, or joined I should say. After all, the wife admittedly had 6 partners before the marriage and the husband acknowledged having at least double that amount. All of a sudden that amounts to calling it safe? Are you kidding me? The numbers just don't add up, I'm afraid. Bottom line is we all need to get tested so that we won't be guessing our status but we will in fact know where we stand. It is the only wise and responsible course of action to take. There is simply no other rational option. We have to get tested and get tested now.

And don't tell me you live in the D.C. area! Statistics show that 1 out of every 20 people in our nation's capital is infected with the HIV VIRUS. Are you kidding me? One out of every twenty people? That means that in every high school and college classroom there is at least one person who has the virus; in every church congregation of 500, there are 25 parishioners who are infected. In every workplace there are 1 in 20 employees in Washington, DC that is infected with HIV. And out of all these cases, the truly sad commentary is that over 80 percent of all those cases in D.C. are African American.

Listen, I'm just the messenger here and I suggest we take the intelligence and govern ourselves accordingly. This means if we are sending our children to colleges in Washington, D.C., we need to make sure they know what they are facing - there especially. They pretty much have to assume when they get there that basically everybody they meet is infected with the HIV Virus or has AIDS. It needs to be assumed everywhere but especially in Washington, D.C.. I'm sorry if that sounds harsh or unfair but we have to change our methods of dealing with our issues. It is imperative that we deal wisely with the problems that plague our communities and protect ourselves in every way available and starting with such basic things as information.

If we have to engage in sexual activity, then it is an absolute requirement that it cost our potential sex partner $100.00 or more to have sex or engage in sexual activity with us. I'm not kidding! We can call it a cover charge, if you will. I know it sounds crazy but we are simply gonna have to demand that they wait at least 30 days and pay a fee of at least $100.00 or more to a competent doctor get the STD/AIDS test where you can have results back and know your status within as little as 3 days. Even then, a condom should be used.

I've gotta give it up to Dr. Creflo and Taffi Dollar in Atlanta for hammering these very facts home from the pulpit. Preachers don't generally want to get involved with topics like this so openly but they have done a phenomenal job. I believe they are even planning to offer testing soon for the entire congregation. I think that's remarkable and maybe other pastors will follow.

It should become the norm in the African American community that if a partner is willing to engage in sexual intercourse with another and does not demand recent STD/AIDS tests results it is assumed that he has AIDS. And we're not referring here to what the proposed partner says was the results but what the actual recent test says.

My suggestion is that this be an adopted standard for Black people that is to be strictly practiced – that is, to never expose ourselves to sexual activity without this requirement. Therefore Sisters, if a brother wants to get all "lovey dovey" and wants to set the mood with candle lights, flowers and music - whereas the prerequisite used to be a condom, brother now needs to do some additional things. He henceforth needs to whip out his recent official doctors papers and THEN maybe he can get it on. Listen, I'm sorry but drastic times call for drastic measures and if abstinence is out the question as it seemingly is for most people, then we have absolutely no other choice but to resort to these desperate but life saving measures.

Speaking of safety, I am obligated to mention that studies have found that while condoms are estimated at being 97% effective in protecting against pregnancy (if used correctly), they are estimated to be only 60% effective in protecting against AIDS and other STD's. I was not aware of these facts until recently as I began digging into statistical analysis available on the subject. Therefore if these reports are accurate, then we have a huge amount to be concerned about when it comes to protecting ourselves and educating our children and loved ones on the issue.

Again, my advice to all would simply be to first of all get tested and prayerfully we are all found to be HIV/Negative and free of any other sexually transmitted diseases. That being the case, we must consider ourselves very fortunate, blessed, lucky – knock on wood- or whatever your flavor. And we have to love and respect ourselves enough to never expose ourselves again to another potentially deadly set of circumstances. Abstinence until marriage is seemingly more and more attractive these days or as Bishop David L. White, Jr. would say, "I guess God was right about this sex topic after all."

Still let me reiterate, before you jump the broom, kiss your bride, or say "I Do," make sure you obtain and carefully examine those certified test results from a licensed physician that we spoke about earlier. That means at the time that the man or woman proposes to his/her mate, the default answer should be changed from, "I Will" to "I will - provided you supply me with the necessary paper-work." "But I'm a virgin," she'd reply. My answer would be, "Great! Then you won't have any problem at all getting a physician to give you a clean bill of health. And by the way, could you get him to certify that virginity claim as well? I'd like to brag on you to my Mom – she'd love that!"

The last point I want to make about this topic is that studies show that out of the staggering 1 million + Americans who are infected with the HIV Virus, about 1/3 of them are not even aware that they have it. So this means that when we ask our partners if they have AIDS, chances are they are gonna say, "No" because they really do not know that they have it. Just as if your partner were to ask YOU if you were HIV Positive you'd more likely than not reply, "NO," when in fact you really do not know. Every single and married person in the United States of America should know of a certainty where they stand on the issue especially those of us who according to recent reports, are at greater risk.

It is essential further that we all know our status because advanced medicine has dramatically improved the quality of life of those who have HIV and later develop AIDS simply by the administration of early treatment. The danger of not knowing robs a person of the benefit of such health care as most only learn of their dire condition when it's basically too late. And remember wishing we don't have doesn't make us not have it. And while I know it is a stretch to think that people will be courageous enough to do it, but once we discover we are infected, not only can we begin to receive treatment ourselves but we should also contact those that we have been with and encourage them to get tested as well – like our spouses!! Therefore if we don't care enough about ourselves, at least get tested for the benefit of the one we love. His or her life may very well be the one we save as while full blown AIDS may never develop from the virus in our bodies, it may be that our spouse who has it too is not so fortunate. I challenge us to be the bigger of the two.

As I write here today, I am one of the many (of us) who simply does not know where I stand but I am going to make a conscious effort to change that. I hereby commit to setting a positive example by leading millions of readers in the fight against AIDS in the Black Community and in America by getting tested. I therefore encourage everyone small and great, rich and poor alike, Super Black or Regular Black to spend the $100 or so and get tested now. Know your status!

Just a few housekeeping issues and we'll wrap it up:

1. Every adult male and female needs to have term life insurance. Period. The amount depends upon our various responsibilities. It is such a disgrace that we die and leave our wives and children with no income or assets, but all the debt load and a funeral bill on top of that. Come on now, that is a disgrace. Term insurance is cheap especially for younger nonsmokers. Lock in for 20 to 30 years before age 36. Wealthy people also are known to establish wealth through life insurance – may sound creepy but legacies of poverty and despair are even more so. Black men under 55 should have at least $500,000 in term coverage for their families.

2. As Black men, we need to kiss our sons and daughters. We must embrace them in our arms often speaking words of inspiration and life into their hearts. They'll believe it and be forced to behave accordingly.

3. Every Black Family needs a library in the home. It can start with a shelf of books in the den but a commitment to reading and acquisition of knowledge beyond school curriculum is a must. Every wealthy family has a library in the home of some type.

Designate a library opposed to the traditional play room. The kids can play outside.

4. No more excuses about can't find a job. If the area that we live in is not thriving or plants shut down, MOVE!

5. We need to pay child support for every child that we've Fathered and on time, regardless. The child didn't ask to be born and it's not their fault that we have to pay. Furthermore, child support is the least we can do as our children need much more.

6. Stop blaming White folks for not wanting us in their neighborhoods when we won't mind the upkeep of our lawns and maintain our property adequately. Many of us keep ragged cars and car motors in the front yard pretending like we are gonna someday restore them. A lot of times it's not that White people don't want us as neighbors because we're Black but due to economics – a lot of them are simply trying to protect their neighborhood's home values. It's not that Blacks and Mexicans bring the value of a neighborhood down so much as it is the behavior and lifestyles of the two. Cut the grass more than once a month and use a weed eater to edge sidewalks and driveways. Trim the hedges more than once a year for crying out loud. And

Mexicans need to put the tortillas and bean sandwich paper in garbage cans instead of in the yard.

7. We must talk to our sons and daughters about sex early on and prepare them for the changes in their bodies that are to occur shortly ahead. We must influence them positively before their peers and society beat us to it. It is disastrous as statistics clearly show to do as we have been doing which is pretending like the issues do not exist. We must teach our daughters to value and respect their bodies and to save themselves for marriage. We must teach our sons to do the same and to respect women and refuse to violate them. We must teach them that it is okay for a man to be clean and pure –free from venereal diseases and aids. For Pete's sake, let's give them a fighting chance and not leave them to the luck of the draw as we were subject.

8. Blacks need to take the necessary steps now to educate ourselves as well our children in financial matters. We must mandate that we read books and become diligent students of financial literacy and practice the application thereof.

9. Every economically challenged Black family with young boys in the home should have a pair of clippers in the house. They cost

about $15 and come with guides which makes cutting hair fool proof. Clippers will save hundreds of dollars a year in hair cuts and give confidence to young boys who otherwise wouldn't have one.

10. Black men please encourage others to pull their britches up on their tails. We've even got 50 and 60 year old men wearing their pants half-way their buttocks. We all know that old men, even Blacks, tend to lose what tail they had when they were young as they age so to try to wear baggy jeans at this stage is just pitiful.

11. If we're gonna put 24" rims on cars, let's at least make sure that the car is worth more than the rims and we can afford to put news tires on the rims every 3-6 months. I'm sure by now we've found out that those dubs wear out new tires about as fast as we can put them on. We've gotta change tires almost every time we change oil.

12. We must be very mindful of our association as we all know that it brings assimilation. The harsh reality is that a lot of us just need to get new friends – individuals that are going in the direction that we are trying to go. And family often times present the greatest stumbling blocks to a person realizing their

dreams and living up to their fullest potential. Close friends and family are often dream killers and the pressure of pleasing them can literally cost us our dreams. We must press on because nobody can help anybody if everybody is broke.

13. Eat healthy. I realize it is deeply rooted in our culture to season food with fat back and hog mog. I realize that Big Momma cooked that way and our daughters were taught to cook a certain way but it's killing us. It's the reason that Blacks suffer disproportionately from diabetes, high blood pressure, high cholesterol, and strokes. We don't have to eat chitterlings, ham hocks, pig's feet, and oxtails any more. Furthermore we should not celebrate the fact that we as an oppressed people were forced to eat these unhealthy left-overs of the slave owners just to survive.

14. Stop renting homes – buy them instead and for less than their fair market values. Renters are consumers who pay Landlords' (like me) mortgages off. I appreciate those who do but you don't have to be one of them.

CHAPTER 6

The Difference Between The Rich And The Poor!

Finally I get an opportunity to lighten up and talk about something that I enjoy without all the friction and uneasiness that Race Relations entail. Believe it or not I do not enjoy being controversial though I often find myself being so. I'd actually prefer like everyone else to be admired and accepted by the masses as the cool guy who represents the opinion of mainstream Americans where nobody who is significant disagrees with me. It's tough going against the grain a lot of times and believe me it gets old and tiresome during the course of it all. But hey, somebody's gotta do it so I assume that fate has drafted me for the job.

Here goes the fun part! I'll begin by asserting affirmatively that no one has an excuse in America to be poor. That's right no excuses whatsoever. If we are of a sane mind and are reasonably healthy with the mobility of our legs, hands, and feet we are in a guaranteed position to not only shun poverty but to lay claim on middle classed income immediately. In chapter 9, I endeavor to share how anyone who desires to do so can earn $50,000.00 a year regardless of one's race, sex, education, or background but here I only seek to discover the root of poverty and lay the foundation for becoming wealthy that is required whatever a person's income.

As I shared earlier in the book, I have been an entrepreneur at heart since as long as I can remember thanks to the positive words imparted by my parents. During the course of my life I have made some observations as it relates to finances and attaining wealth that I deem worthy of mention in hopes that they will inspire someone else to reach beyond the grips of poverty and embark on the rewarding journey toward financial freedom. Even if you have no desire to become rich or financially independent, certainly you don't desire to be poor. Because many people don't know where they actually stand as it relates to income classes in America, I thought it would be beneficial to provide the poverty guidelines as presented by the United States Department of Human Services.

2008 HHS Poverty Guidelines

Persons In Household Only 1 Wage Earner		48 Contiguous States & D.C.	Alaska	Hawaii
1	$5.00 Hr	$10,400	$13,000	$11,960
2	$6.74 Hr	14,000	17,500	16,100
3	$8.50 Hr	17,600	22,000	20,240
4	$10.20 Hr	21,200	26,500	24,380
5	$11.93 Hr	24,800	31,000	28,520
6	$13.66 Hr	28,400	35,500	32,660
7	$15.39 Hr	32,000	40,000	36,800
8	$17.12 Hr	35,600	44,500	40,940
		3,600	4,500	4,140

SOURCE: *Federal Register*, Vol. 73, No. 15, January 23, 2008, pp. 3971–3972

Again, it is vitally important to know where we stand instead of simply winging it - or worse, not caring at all. I actually disagree with those figures and strongly feel they should be 10 to 15% higher across the board given the rise of gas and energy prices. For example take an average budget of the single mom who has two school aged children in the home:

Income	Basic Monthly Expenses	
$8.50 Per Hour	FICA Taxes	113.00
	Federal/State Taxes	-0-
X	Rent	599.00
	Utilities	250.00
40 Hours Per Week =	Car Payments	-0-
$340.00 Per Week	Life/Health Ins.	199.00
X 52 Weeks =	Grocery	300.00
$17,680.00 Gross Annually	Gas/Taxi Fare	150.00
	Clothing Allowance	50.00
	Tithes/Gifts To Faith	-0-

Entertainment	-0-
Credit Cards	-0-
	$1,661.00
	X 12 Mos.

$17,680.00 Gross Annually	Minimum Actual Expenses $19,932.00

DEFICIT $2,252.00

As you can see from the above example with barely allowing only the basic accommodations, the single mom comes up short nearly two hundred bucks a month of making ends meet. Bare in mind we only budgeted the family $599.00 a month in rent so you can imagine the apartment complex she must live in as you'd be hard pressed to find decent three bedroom units nowadays for under $700.00. Notice also that there is no room for car payments, credit card bills, or even giving a few dollars to a local church. Transportation budget is strictly limited to commuting to and from work and with those figures her workplace has to be in pretty close proximity. With a budget like this there is absolutely no room for anything at all to go wrong. In short, it cannot be sustained on anywhere near that $17,600.00 income suggested by the United States Department of Human Services. Even the $19,932.00 annual income that we displayed in our budget is unrealistic.

I am very proud of the fact that I have endeavored from the very beginning of this project to provide a relevant reading that provides real life solutions to ordinary people's problems in addition to those of extraordinary status. That can only be accomplished when those who embark upon this reading can take the words from the pages and execute them in their own lives and those around them and get the results that were represented therein. Only then would I have achieved my purpose with this calligraphy.

Often times when reading self help books, the guys who are starting from the ground floor with next to nothing to begin with seem so far detached from actually realizing the product of what they read. Writers oftentimes speak of accomplishing successes of epic proportions which certainly intrigue the ordinary guy but more frequently than not it remains merely wishful thinking or at best something that can be possible only in the distant future. You will discover in this chapter inspiration and ideas for attaining extreme prosperity but I purposed to ensure that ordinary workers struggling to make ends meet with a minimum wage job can radically change their circumstances in the meantime.

I realize that it's quite a challenge trying to convince the guy working for $6.55 per hour at the local lumber yard that he can be a multi-million dollar business man when he's currently working 12 hour days to make ends meet. That guy, though inspired, cannot fathom how it is possible at this point in his life to make a change and at the same time keep a roof over his family's head, keep the lights on in the house, and keep food on the table. Where does the guy start we often wonder - and don't shoot the same old dry "take up a trade at the local community college" line. And I am all for school – high school, state universities as well as community colleges. But give me something I can subscribe to now that will change my circumstances in the immediate to near future, for Pete's sake!

The difference, as I see it, between the Rich and the Poor in the United States or anywhere in the world for that matter is simply KNOWLEDGE or lack thereof as it relates to finances. I have said it once and will reiterate it again and again until it sinks in the minds of those of us who fail to realize that ignorance of basic financial principles are to blame for the lack and poverty in our lives. Show me a wealthy person and I will show you a guy who possesses distinct knowledge of and properly applies certain principles of finance that produces increase in his life.

And likewise, if you show me a man who is poor and destitute, I will show you a guy who though he may be proficient in many other areas, is ignorant as it pertains to financial literacy. Am I trying to tell you that poor people are ignorant? Absolutely! The vast majority of poor in this country and around the world are that way largely due to ignorance where finances are concerned –not ignorance, in general.

Now I know by this time I have ruffled a few feathers among my constituency to say the least but please hear me out before you write me off as a brute – hear me out for a moment. In order to really absorb and realize any meaningful benefit to anything I am about to share in this section it is so material that we concede the fact that we have not studied nor have we been taught financial literacy by the educational system, our parents, or anyone else. And as a result, we are ignorant of the subject and have made a mess of our finances. Our total outlook where money is concerned and how to obtain, keep, and grow it is completely flawed. We don't understand it except for the fact that we need lots of it and cannot function effectively without it. Now if you already have tons of it where money is no object for you then obviously this section will be of little value. However if the opposite is true then this segment, if approached objectively and honestly, could very well change your life forever both in the short term and for years to come.

CONSUMERS

From the time that many of us were born, we observed all the wrong examples about finances from our parents to friends and family. I don't know about you but my parents were ordinary people who struggled to make ends meet and basically lived from paycheck to paycheck. This was quite evident to me even as a young child. As best as I can remember, I do not recall anyone ever actually sitting down with me and teaching me anything at all about finances.

I, like many Americans, pretty much learned on the go obviously by observing those who were closest to me. What I distinctly remember is that there was never enough money to go around. I also remember bill collectors calling and late notices in the mail. I recall so vividly how my Dad almost on a weekly basis borrowed $100 or so from my Uncle Bay Bro down the street trying to bridge the gap between his weekly bills and his paycheck. These images, while there was never a word spoken about it directly to me, played a major role in how I viewed and approached finances from that time forth. And I realize and appreciate that my Mother and Father did the very best they could with the knowledge that they had at the time.

It wasn't until several months ago that I began to examine and change the way my own children viewed and learned finances. The truth is that everybody is forced to learn it one way or another and it's just that many of us learn through watching the poor financial habits of others around us. This of course develops wrong thinking which leads to wrong practices which ultimately leads to financial ruin. We find this to be the case even as we begin to earn significantly more money. When the foundation of anything is flawed, everything that comes afterward is likely to be also which is a certain recipe for failure.

When I began to judge critically the examples that I was setting before my children, it didn't take very long for me to recognize that I was setting them up to fail. Whether we realize it or not, kids are very bright and they are constantly observing us and can hardly wait to mimic what they see demonstrated before them – good or bad. It's truly amazing to discover that they will almost by rote duplicate the financial habits displayed by their parents and others they grow up around.

One of the absolute worst things that we teach them, along with society and our educational system, is to be CONSUMERS. Just stop and think about it. From a small child we are given a false lesson in finance by having a dollar bill politely given to us along with the expert advice, from the philanthropist who gave it, to go and spend the whole thing on a toy or some cookies. Thus, we are programmed from a very early age to consume every dollar we get our hands on and are encouraged to do so at our earliest convenience. Say Amen if you can. Many of you are laughing or shaking your heads in agreement because you know it's right. We are taught the moment we get some money in our hands that the most expedient thing to do is go and spend it – not some of it, but every dime of it. This is what we have been training our children to do generation after generation and it's time we correct it, but beginning with ourselves. Easier said than practiced, I assure you.

Wait a minute, though. That's only one aspect of the problem though notably a major component. Another is the other extreme which is simply being obsessed with saving it all and refusing to consider anything else. Now granted, this is a far better fault than the previous because at least when it's all said and done at the end of the year or at the age of retirement there is a nest egg to draw from. However as we will find later in this chapter there is an equilibrium to the two that has largely to do with our way of thinking when it comes to finances. Wrong information produces this wrong thinking which in turn produces wrong actions which of course breeds poverty, lack, financial ruin and everything else that's associated with failure.

Instead of teaching our children to become consumers we should be educating them from early childhood to become intelligent investors. The investor's mindset is that perfect balance between the Consumer and the Chronic Saver. We must come to understand that the mindset of either of these three will ultimately determine their approach toward finances and that their decisions hence will be governed thereby.

Financial literacy or independence is not a phenomenon. It's really truly simple in its make up. I mean it's not rocket science! You do not have to be a very smart person to attain it and unlike the field of science, law, or medicine you don't have to go to school forever and gain 3 or 4 degrees to attain it. The problem is the same as I suggested to us earlier and that is we are just plain ignorant of the principles that govern success as it pertains to finances. I didn't say we were ignorant in general – that would be a serious problem. However I do suggest that we are ignorant in this subject and it is obvious.

Donald Trump, though he is a financial genius in his own right, is probably ignorant as it relates to Rocket Science. And whereas his buddy Robert Kiyosaki is proficient and renowned in Corporate Cash Flow Concepts, he probably is ignorant in a host of different areas such as computer science, global warming and US foreign policy. He may actually be an expert in all these areas as well but the point is that nobody knows everything. We must accept the fact that we are lacking in certain areas and opposed to justifying or masking our ignorance we need to properly correct it through education and the reprogramming of our thinking.

Let's define the term Consumer. Webster's dictionary defines a consumer as, "one who consumes." That doesn't sound too bad, does it? That is, until you research the root word which is consume and it is there we discover what it truly means to consume, or rather to be a consumer. Again, Webster's dictionary defines the root word consume as follows: **"to do away with completely: destroy; to spend wastefully: squander;**

to use up; to eat or drink especially in great quantity; to engage fully; to waste or burn away." So there we have it – we get mad when I suggest that we are ignorant concerning finances yet we don't mind when Corporate America distastefully and openly refers to us all as CONSUMERS. In other words we are squanderers, wasters, destroyers... you get the picture!

So as defined, we are not consumers just because we use or spend money- that is, as long as we do not use it up completely. Common sense dictates that everyone rich and poor alike has to USE it but the rich just don't practice using it all up. Likewise we are not consumers simply because we use goods and services as the rich just as others have to do the same. Only the rich differ in that they don't waste, squander, or over-indulge to depletion of all of their resources as we oftentimes do. Ah ha! We might just be on to something here. As we have discovered, it doesn't seem on the surface that it would be that big of an adjustment to posture our thinking and practices after the financially independents of the world opposed to the financially destitute.

Here is a list of bad habits that we were taught as children growing up that still haunt many of us to this very day:

1. Spending every dollar we get.
2. Never setting aside any money for savings.
3. Opposed to the idea of investing a portion of our money.
4. Overspending and writing bad checks.
5. Maxing out credit cards.
6. Accepting any and every extension of credit offered.

7. Paying bills late.
8. Not paying bills at all that are not detrimental.
9. Not giving regularly.
10. Spending to keep up with the Joneses.
11. Bad credit – low fico scores.
12. Renting opposed to Buying.
13. Seeking only Linear Income v/s passive and residual

As we can clearly see from this list, that any one of these bad habits can lead to one struggling financially regardless of the amount of income produced. These financial practices were developed over many years of watching our parents and those around us and they of course observed the same from their parents. And tragically the cycle continues on today and our precious children are being instructed in finance the very same way. Again, financial literacy is really very easy to obtain but once we've been indoctrinated for so long into a certain way of thinking and behaving as it relates to money, we find it extremely difficult to break these habits as they are operating on automatic pilot so to speak. We find ourselves caught up in the rat race of life and on the tread mill of despair, on the road to no where.

The opposite is true for those who grew up in well to do affluent households where the parents displayed fiscal responsibility. The children brought up in this environment netted the benefit of observing their parents' choice of professions, spending, saving, and investing habits. But unlike the previous example what is embedded in their psyche are habits that lead to wealth, financial literacy, and the natural development of practices conducive to success where money is concerned. During the course of twenty (20) years or more all they have ever seen was the Father write out bills and send them off on time every month. Never once could they remember a time when a bill collector called and hearing the Mom explaining why she hadn't paid the mortgage payment on time. It would be completely foreign to them to even think of not paying the utility bill on time or for any reason having to borrow from Peter to pay Paul because they were so overextended and couldn't make ends meet.

After having been exposed to only these positive principals all their lives it is highly doubtful that they will change this behavior when they are finally on their own. And of course, their children will enjoy the same experience which produces generation after generation of financial literacy and successful behavior that becomes perpetual. Below you will discover an example of the strict budget this family followed along with other notable dictates practiced that I recommend we incorporate as our very own.

1. Allocates Religiously 35% Of Gross Income as follows:

    A. Tithes/Gifts   10%

    B. Long Term Savings   10%

    C. Short Term Savings   10%

    D. Household Savings   3%

    E. Emergency Savings   2%

2. Allocates Remaining 65% As follows:

    A. FICA Taxes   7.65%

         Federal/ State Taxes   (Varies)

    B. Mortgage (P&I, Ins./Taxes)   24 %

    C. Transportation (Pays cash for cars)   0%

    D. Utilities, Food, Insurances,   33%
         Entertainment, Clothing, Etc.

3. Pays Credit Card Balances In Full Monthly.

4. Always pays bills on time.

5. Owns primary home and rental property as well.

6. Purposely Maintains a 740 or above FICO score.

Please note that the standard detail above is one that is universal and not confined to one income class or family over another. Here are principles that if followed will guarantee financial independence on every level and if adhered to yield over 1 to 3 Million in cash over 30 years. And bear in mind that the lower figure of $1 Million applies to the lower end family earning only $36,000 per year. That is poverty level income for two wage earners with 3 children according to the HHS Chart – each parent with a low level job making $8.50 an hour each.

The key to it all is that we have to stop the destructive practice we learned as children which is consuming every dollar we get our hands on. According to the budget utilized by the successful family, the $8.50 an hour workers would basically need to operate on 65% of their income thereby saving and investing the other 25% (with remaining 10% charitable). Let's examine it on paper and see how it plays out in a real life situation.

HOUSEHOLD BUDGET #1

Total Monthly Income For Household = **$2,946**

Mandatory Deductions (35%)		**Basic Monthly Expenses (65%)**	
Tithes/Gifts (10%)	$295	FICA Taxes (7.65%)	226.00
Long Term Savings	295	Tithes/Gifts (10%)	
Short Term Savings	295	Federal/State Taxes	-0-
Household Savings	89	Mortgage (24%)	708.00
Emergency	59	Utilities	175.00
		Grocery	300.00
	$1,033	Car Payments	-0-
		Life/Health Ins.	204.00
Total Cash Saved Monthly =	$679	Auto Gas	150.00
Total Cash Saved Yearly=	$8,148	Clothing Allowance	50.00
Total Cash Saved 5 Years=	$40,740	Entertainment	50.00
Total Cash Saved 30 Years=	$244,440	Cable / Internet	50.00
		Credit Card Interest	-0-
			$1,913.00

Figuring Compounded Interest with principal of $244,440 over 30 year period at a modest 9% average rate, principal will yield $866,194 for total of **$1,110,634.**

If a person learned nothing else from this book, it would be more than the equivalency of a college education if they would just learn and master the mechanics of the Household Budget described in this chapter. I think it is truly fascinating yet very simple in its ideology. The lack of understanding the basics of a personal household budget is the reason why many of us have such a difficult time financially. If we were to poll the average person in this country, I am certain that we will find astounding numbers of us who have never taken the time to learn the principles of a household budget. Many of us have never seen one and even more have never actually prepared or adhered to one. And I'm not talking about balancing our checkbooks or checking the bank account to see how much is available to spend at the grocery store on any given visit. What I am speaking of here is a comprehensive budget or plan of spending that governs one's financial affairs consistently and serves as the umpire where the family's checkbook is concerned. Webster's dictionary defines a budget as, " a statement of the financial position of an administration for a definite period of time based on estimates of expenditures during the periods and proposal for financing them; a plan for the coordination of resources and expenditures; the amount of money that is available for, required for, or assigned to a particular purpose."

Most of us are intelligent enough to know that it is vitally necessary to have and operate on a budget but simply are trained to avoid them at all costs. I think a lot of times we do not want to face the reality of just how insufficient our income truly is. We'd much rather operate our finances off the cuff when all the while knowing we are just kidding ourselves. I must reiterate once again that we have been programmed into this wrecklessness all of our lives. We have been hard wired to over-indulge and exceed all limitations whatsoever where money is concerned.

I'd like to rescind a statement that I made previously which suggested that we are taught as children to spend every dime of what is put into our hands. I have to admit that that is an inadequate statement. It's just not true. We'd actually be better off if it were the truth but it just is not. Truth of matter is that we are taught to spend MORE than we actually have and for some strange reason while doing so, psyche ourselves out into thinking that there's actually more that will come available to make up the difference. We pretend like we really don't know how much money we actually make and have available to spend. You see, making an actual budget does away with this charade.

Think about it, Uncle Gertrude gives us $5.00 as a kid and Mom takes us to the store to buy a toy. Now there are hundreds of toys in the toy store that can be bought for $5.00 and we'd have change left over for candy, too. But what do we do? We go and pick out a Tonka truck that costs $6.99 and we take it to our parents knowing dog gone well that we don't have enough money to buy it. If we were really mistaken and didn't know, we certainly wouldn't have brought an item that was that close to the amount we actually had available to spend. If we were really that innocent (or ignorant) we'd roll an $80.00 bicycle to the checkout line instead. How is it that when we go over the amount that we have, it's usually not that much beyond? I'll tell you why – it's because we have been trained that we can always get away with going over, but just a little bit.

The problem is that a little bit becomes more and more. So what happens is we take the Tonka truck to Mom who is patiently waiting at the counter and hand it to her, hoping for the best. More than likely our mothers would give us that evil eye and maybe fuss for a moment or two but hey, the upgraded toy is well worth the rebuke. The same goes for the candy store, the clothing store, the shoe store, as well as the sporting goods store. For twenty years or more these lessons and principles of finances have been instilled in us and tend to operate innately. If the state of mind were not so pitiful it might even be amusing but when we really stop and examine the behavior, it's just plain ridiculous. We as parents teach our children that it is okay to over-indulge and spend recklessly when we succumb to their impetuous demands.

Calling our attention back to the household budget chart, we learn fundamental lessons that we have been deprived of for all this time. One of the most powerful reproofs of all is simply that we do not have as much to spend of our paychecks as we thought we did. I know it sounds elementary but we haven't really grasped it. We just don't understand finances as we should but have become fairly good at pretending that we do.

Just because our paychecks at the end of the work week says $500.00 at the bottom in the net pay box doesn't really mean we have $500.00 available to spend. Remember the definition of budget; " the amount of money that is available for, required for, or assigned to a particular purpose." The proper course of action to take once money has come into our hands whether by paycheck or mere gift is to refer to the governor of our money, or umpire thereof – if you will. We must default to the budget! I realize that high heels and pocketbooks are the first things that may come to mind (for the ladies) and perhaps electronics and sports (for the fellows) but it is the governor of our finances who makes the final call.

Notice that, if properly followed, a whopping 35% of our entire take is immediately subtracted and should automatically be treated as if it does not exist. This unfortunately is where the majority of our fallouts occur. If we could get this one aspect of our finances right, we could really do whatever we thought we were big and bad enough to do with the other. It wouldn't make a whole lot of difference because mastering the first portion would ensure three things. First, it would guarantee a millionaire retirement at age 55. Two, it would ensure that the person would never have to borrow money to make ends meet. And finally, it would make the subscriber feel like they're pretty well off (or feel good) because they'd always know that they are not "broke." They will be keenly aware that significant resources are stored up in the bank or brokerage house.

Don't laugh, number 3 is very important! One of the main negatives of being poor or without is the reality of knowing that not only can we not pay our bills but also the fact that we don't have a dime in the bank, that is unclaimed. But I assure you that if we can get over the first hump (it's easier if we're just getting started without the family, big house, boat, dog . . . you know), the rest is a piece of cake.

The bottom line is that we only have 65% of what we thought we had – to work with. That's right, when we give our children $5.00 they have to realize at their young ripe age that they really do not have $5.00. What they really have is $3.25 ! It's really actually fun to teach the principle to children because they will grasp it and buy into the concept rather quickly especially once they see how much they are actually accumulating as a result. Besides, it's easier for them to understand that the excess candy and soda pops were vain anyhow - after all, it is us parents who were pushing these negative practices on them in the first place. They would probably be wondering anyhow why it took us so long to figure this stuff out.

Getting back to the 35% rule, we all were under the false assumption that we had all that money at our disposal. Violating this fundamental principle of finance is what classifies individuals as CONSUMERS. Remember, a consumer is one who consumes and to consume, we've learned, means "to do away with completely; to squander; to use up; to destroy; " according to Webster's. Making this minor adjustment is what ultimately determines what class of people we are gonna represent and what options are gonna be available to us in life. It will ultimately decide whether we will be rich or poor.

When we take the time to actually consider our practices we really ought to feel pretty silly. We pretend that we have more than we actually have in a fruitless effort to impress our family and friends with the new cars, the new boat, the new shoes, the new house, and the new furniture. Our family and friends know that we're in debt up to our eyeballs anyhow and that financial collapse is eminent. Even still they in turn do the same things to try to keep up with us and get into the same dilemma.

My son gets a new dirt bike and your son becomes sad. Certainly you can't have your son sad so you go and put a $2,000.00 better dirt bike on your credit card to even the score. The same is true with Christmas, Easter, and school shopping. We max the credit cards out and get more credit until finally they won't give us any more and the reality sets in that we simply cannot afford all this stuff. Everybody knows that it's all just vanity anyway and mere illusions, but it doesn't change anything.

At this point we're miserable and the children still aren't satisfied. The wife still wants more and more clothes, shoes, and hair dos and the creditor wants all that money back that he so graciously loaned us. But the problem is now that we just don't have it and can no longer pay. That 750 credit score that made it possible to acquire all of those nice trinkets is shot to pieces. We'd be lucky if it were a 475 at this point and wouldn't dare check it for fear of going into depression at the results.

The paychecks remain the same and here comes the late fees, over the limit fees, the cut off fees, the reconnection fees and all sorts of other kind of fees. Nobody dare answers the phone anymore and believe me it's ringing off the hook. Do you really think the kids don't know why we won't answer the telephone? I know we told them that we don't have time to talk to all those friends calling or that it's nobody but those worrisome telemarketers. Come on now – they are smarter than that just like we were and knew the real reason why Mom and Dad wouldn't always answer the phone. And do you think they don't know what we're doing when a creditor somehow actually catches us answering the phone and we tip toe out of the room and begin to whisper looking over our shoulders? Of course they know and it's class in session – home schooling 101 and I assure you they will get straight A's in how to wreck their financial future unless something or somebody intervenes and stops this madness.

Thirty-five percent 35% of our take home doesn't exist. We should have it deducted and taken out of the equation right off the top just like FICA, federal, and state income taxes are. The government has already figured out that the majority of us wouldn't have sense enough to realize that we could not just consume all of that money we get every week or month in our paychecks. As a result the federal and state government helps themselves by taking their taxes right off the top before we get our hands on it. They were wise enough to know that if we touched it, it would be slim pickings trying to get it back as we would certainly consume it.

Investors and/or business owners are not treated like that by the government, as we will discover later. They trust, for the most part, these guys to send theirs in on their own accord a couple times a year opposed to every time they get a check, as they do regular employees.

Investors and business owners at least get to touch and feel the money they worked so hard for at least for a little while. Employees don't get that benefit and never see it. It goes right through them.

We learn that by giving priority to and properly appropriating the first 35% of our wages we set ourselves up for success while constantly reminding ourselves that we are not consumers. The first 10% allocated for **Tithes or Gifts** are done so in acknowledgement of the fact that many Americans, African Americans especially, are members of local assemblies, mosques, or churches where it is customary to tithe or gift an estimated 10% of one's income to those institutions. Studies show additionally that giving a portion of one's livelihood to charity is actually good for us mentally and serves as food for the soul. I agree with that as it serves a great deterrent from becoming self-centered and otherwise indifferent to causes other than our own.

Another 10% is assigned to **Long Term Savings** such as a retirement account of some sort, perhaps the employee's 401k or IRA. Whatever the case, 10% is provided for saving/investing over the long term and is not to be mettled with at all.

Further, an extra 10% is allocated for **Short Term** investments but what differs with this particular account is that it is to be separate and apart from the previous and controlled and directed more liberally by the individual. This account will be utilized for more aggressive yet sound investing such as rental property acquisition. I expect to deal more extensively with this topic later.

Next there is the matter of **Household Savings** which would be an account that is to remain for the most part a liquid account in which a modest 3% of earnings would be deposited. This is not an account to be dipping and dabbing into, though it is sure to be awful tempting, I will admit. This is that account that makes us feel good – the pride account that whereas our peers and neighbors will look like they have some money, we on the other hand will actually have some readily available – not to consume, however. Remember, it's only feel good money, for illusional purposes only. One would be surprised at how fast it will accumulate though it represents only a small percentage. A continual dripping, however, can run a bathtub over.

And finally we come to the last of the mandatory first to be subtracted from our earnings which is the **Emergency Savings**. We have properly allocated 2% of our checks to facilitate any emergencies that may arise from time to time. Now we are not providing for Big Mac attacks or Macy's once a year shoe sales. This account will be a separate account in the event something unexpected comes up that was not provided for in the original budget. I should mention that whenever possible, we should try to figure other ways to fund such occurrences especially insignificant ones so that we may build the account up to levels over time that will accommodate a substantial emergency (God-forbid) should one occur.

I cannot stress enough how simply embracing these practices as our very own will completely transform our financial conditions and truly reprogram our thinking and future outlook where money is concerned. We'd be pleasantly surprised at how much better and less stressed we would be just by knowing that we actually have a savings now. May not be much initially but a clear $25.00 would be a great accomplishment for many. I remember it being for me when I first subscribed to the undertaking and I recall very vividly how excited my children were when they began – that is, after first of all getting over the shock of realizing that they no longer had what they thought they had when they got a piece of money. And I won't pretend, I don't have such a great head start on anybody but I can say that I have started and that I am faithful to the concept along with my family and we refuse to turn back. No excuses!

To be fair, I have to disclose to everyone something my wife challenged me on that a lot of guys writing self help books just don't want to deal with. I must admit that I was a bit uncomfortable with the confrontation at first myself. The question she asked when I was explaining to her where I was with this writing is this. "What is the remedy for people who have already messed up and are in debt up to their necks right now where they find it virtually impossible to implement your so-called 35% remedy?"

That, my friends (as Senator John McCain would say), is a very smart question. My wife doesn't mind challenging me and calling me out on the carpet about issues. I find it frustrating at times wishing she would simply go with the flow or "roll with me" as I would often encourage her. But it's a tough question and one that needs to be addressed as a large percentage of the people who read these types of books are in this very dilemma and are screaming for a way out. If she were reading this section right now, she'd be interrupting saying, "Look, bottom line me – are you gonna deal with it or are you gonna be like most everyone else who seem to write to other people who are just like they are, only to leave the ones who really need the information no better off (from an applicable perspective) than they were when they picked the book up to begin with?" Well, I have to admit that she's right as she is 75% of the time!

Here we go. First, let's go ahead and get right to worst case scenario from the gitty up. This is the family that is just messed up altogether financially and we all know why. "See what had happened was. . . " Yeah, we know. The same thing that happened to the rest of us. Teachers encouraged us all through school to study hard, go to college, be a doctor, or lawyer, engineer – you name it. Here's a family where both parents are college grads – Dad earns a decent $40,000 a year and Mom earns a respectable (I guess) $32,000 for a combined total of $72,000.00.

Everything was lovely at first but like most others found themselves in life's same ole rat race. Every bill that is not directly drawn from the checking account is paid late every month. The mortgage is much more than they can afford and has been over 30 days late pretty consistently. They pay the utility bill a day before the cut off date every single month and the two car payments are behind and are always a step away from repossession. The wife, however, is constantly in touch with the banks explaining and begging them to hold off until the next payday, so they have been able to keep their heads just above water. Oh, did I mention that they are caught up in the pay day loan charade and have had several checks to bounce as a result?

I know it's a given and doesn't need to be mentioned but we know all the credit cards are maxed out and 6 of the 9, between the two of them, are over the limit and 3 of them have already been charged off. The husband's fancy SUV needs tires and the wife's C-Class Mercedes has already missed 4 scheduled oil changes and needs a brake job soon. And don't even ask about credit scores because you know they are both in the tank – add both of them together and you couldn't get a 700.

Nobody ever observing this beautiful family of 6 would ever guess that things were this bad. After all, they live in a very nice neighborhood, $250,000 home, 2 late model automobiles, manicured lawn, a dog, and a gold fish. Their children wear the latest fashions, have the latest bicycles, scooters, and play stations. The two boys keep fresh hair cuts and you know the two daughters keep the hair done (or hair did) along with the finger nails and eyebrow arches.

This family no doubt is envied by the family who lives on the other side of town who's parents earn half of the wages represented in this case. You can just imagine how the children of the other family only dream of living the life of these kids. What they don't know is while they wrongly assume that this wasteful family is rich and well to do, their own family actually surpasses them financially by leaps and bounds. The children of the fiscally conservative take for granted the peace and financial security that they enjoy at home not realizing that the stress of money problems in the other has pushed them to point of separation.

Take a look at the financial situation of the family of 6 that has gotten uncontrollably out of whack. I have attempted to put it in budget form so that we may properly evaluate it and offer remedies for correction. "What is your remedy for a mess this extreme?" my wife would ask. I wish I could use the answer that my nephew Jamonty would use when he was younger. Whenever he was asked how he was able to solve a problem or perform a task so well, he would ALWAYS reply with such confidence one word, "EAASY!"

But unfortunately I am not as bright as my nephew is so I'm afraid this situation is gonna require much more creativity, labor, and discipline than most people are willing to sign up for. I bet you, though, kids such as Jamonty given the proper basics of financial literacy, would in fact come to very simple and easy solutions to adult problems like these. In fact, what I recommend is the best thing a family can do to begin to get out of a mess like this is to exercise full disclosure to the kids. Go ahead and level with them and allow them to help with solutions in resolving the problems - and do it as a family. But no, we'd much rather continue to try to hide it from them as if they weren't smart enough to already know that we're in over our heads.

We did this in our own family when we finally decided to get out of the rat race and we were surprised to learn that our children first of all already knew the deal and secondly were very eager to make the necessary adjustments to get out of the situation. Therefore, we successfully began the process of killing two birds with one stone. Thus, we were correcting our financial mess and at the same time educating our children properly where finances are concerned, ensuring that they'd never have to fall into the same disheartening predicament. However, most families would rather keep pretending which a lot of times just ends up in broken homes through divorce and continued irresponsible financial behavior. All the while the children suffer and receive proficient training in how to fail financially and repeat the cycle all over again.

HOUSEHOLD BUDGET #2

(ROUNDED)

Income			Basic Monthly Expenses	
			FICA Taxes	650.00
			Federal/State Taxes	400.00
$40,000			Mortgage	2,150.00
$32,000			Utilities	350.00
$72,000	Annual Gross		Car Payments	1,250.00
$6,000 Monthly Gross			Life/Health Ins.	500.00
			Grocery	500.00
Tithes/Gifts		-0-	Gas	250.00
Long Term Savings		-0-	Clothing Allowance	50.00
Short Term Savings		-0-	Entertainment	-0-
Household Savings		-0-	Credit Cards	1,200.00
Emergency Savings		-0-	Cable/Internet	100.00
TOTAL SAVINGS		-0-		$7,400.00
				X 12 Mos.

$72,000.00 Gross Annually | **Minimum Actual Expenses $88,800.00**

ANNUAL DEFICIT $-16,800.00

Notice here in this budget that things appear just hopeless. We can clearly see that there is simply not enough income to sustain the monthly expenses that this family has to dish out every month and it is a sad commentary. However, a large percentage of Americans Black and White are in this predicament – some even worse. Right now, I'll go ahead and tell you that there is no EASY fix, though there are remedies available. Let's deal with a couple of them.

First step is for us to realize and take ownership of the fact that we screwed up big time. Note, I said that we have to accept and acknowledge the reality of our mistakes and see them for what they are. This is so important. Most people would simply like to skip over this portion and just go right into what they need to do to correct the issues but we cannot do that in this case. We have to understand that we got here because of a mindset (or way of thinking) that is not transformed as easily as we may think. Remember, we've been thinking and behaving this way for twenty (20) years or more and basically everywhere we turn and everyone that we see or associate with shares and displays the same dysfunctional behavior as it relates to finances. If we just jump into the application of the things that correct or offset the core problem without properly dealing with the root, the chances of us reverting back to those values and repeating the causes are inescapable. It's like in Alcohol Anonymous where participants are required to face their condition head on and opposed to proceeding ahead in the attempt to quit drinking, they are forced to come to grips and admit to themselves – many for the first time ever- that they are indeed alcoholics.

You see, we have been pretending all this time that we are financially responsible and can actually afford all of this stuff. We have been playing make pretend with our friends, family members, neighbors, and fellow workers on the job. Our many fancy cars and homes were so called proof that we had made it, or were otherwise well off and it was important that everyone knew it. We have to come to accept that this way of thinking is just ridiculous and plainly irresponsible. We have to get it out in the open and admit that our behavior in regards to operating without a budget is just stupid. Nobody wants to be stupid on purpose or behave that way intentionally but it is quite easy to do when a person tricks himself into believing that his activity is the opposite. If we'd be honest with ourselves in examining our actions in retrospect, we would discover that we have been actively practicing this and merely blocking out the reality of our lack of education and understanding as it relates to finances.

We knew goodness well that we did not have $500.00 extra available to spend on toys and games at Christmas time. The light bill was overdue and the mortgage was already late. Nevertheless there was no way we could go through the holidays without making sure our kids had at least as many gizmos and gadgets that their friends were sure to have. We have to understand that our conditions resulted not as a result of a mere mistake or intermittent mis-judgement here or there, but they were the just reward of our psychotic behavior in regard to our finances. We have to face up to that.

I realize that the term psychotic seems a bit extreme but I took the time to define the word and found that it was very appropriate. Dictionary.com's thesaurus ascribed adjectives such as, "**disordered, demented, crazy, loony,**" oh, and "**nuts.**" Webster's characterizes the term as a person which, "**seems to have difficulty distinguishing reality from fantasy,**" and then referred me to the term lunatic. I didn't even examine that one because I knew where I was headed and did not want to seem any more vile than I'm certain I already have.

I thought it only appropriate to require that we recognize the behavior for what it is and take a good look in the mirror at ourselves. That person described or defined above by reputable dictionaries – in my opinion- accurately represents the way of thinking and dysfunctional lifestyles that many of us fully endorse. I cannot imagine that any reasonable person on the planet would ever think of conscionably behaving in this manner. However many of us do it every single day of our lives and it is not limited to any particular age, race, religion, or even professional status. This state of being claims participants not only of the poor and disadvantaged but similarly doctors, lawyers, senators, and sadly even Accountants and C.P.A.'s. We have to come to understand that it is not an issue of financial lack but more so one of financial ignorance and judgement. And while accountants and certified public accountants are without excuse because they understand the concept more than any, it goes to show that even with learning the proper principles one can still choose to behave irresponsibly. Therefore changing our fundamental way of thinking regarding finances is key to sustaining financial health once we are relieved of the hold that this psychotic behavior has had on us all these years.

Bottom line is that operating without a sound budget in life is just plain, "NUTS!" We should be embarrassed. It is only after this that we are ready to dig in and explore our options of correction.

It is imperative that every single person alive create, understand, and operate on a budget. Everybody has to have a budget. It doesn't matter if we are poor and only earn seven thousand ($7,000.00) a year or a billionaire who earns or has income of ten billion ($10,000,000,000.00) a year. A budget in either case is essential to creating and sustaining any degree of financial health. Nobody earns enough money to operate without a budget of some form obviously because we can always spend more than we make. Even billionaires bounce checks and can't pay their bills. Don't believe it? I'll provide a few examples.

Major corporations file for bankruptcy every year because they, in short, spend or pay out more than they take in. Small businesses go out of business every day because they are unable to produce enough income faster than they are spending. It's a very difficult task to manage keeping income ahead of spending or expenses as we often experience in our own households.

However, the most significant example of all is that of our country's state. The United States brings in hundreds of billions of dollars in income each year yet we manage to find a way to spend it all and billions more! WOW! Everyone knows that America is an exceedingly RICH country yet we overspend by billions and are in financial trouble right now. So I guess then that the ultimate example of this irresponsible behavior that we have participated in all this time is personified by one of the richest, most sought after women in the world, AMERICA! Don't follow her example.

Well there's the uncontroverted proof that no matter how much income a person or entity may boast, one can always find a way to spend more than that amount. And remember the revelation we received that properly described the actions of those of us who practice this type of behavior, right? Right. Therefore, we all agree that creating, understanding, and most of all strictly adhering to a sound budget is paramount.

Now that we have laid a firm foundation for the transformation of our thinking, we can now get down to the attack stage. First thing we do at this stage of the game is what Arnold Schwarzenegger is getting so much heat about in California. And I realize that it is not very popular, but I applaud the governor for taking the better of the only two options he has – cutting costs or raising income which is raising taxes. Now I am in no way endorsing one way or the other nor approving of any particular cuts he is proposing. I have not examined any very closely nor do I profess to be qualified to do so. After all, I profess to be no financial genius. Notwithstanding, it doesn't take a C.P.A. to figure out that if proposed expenditures exceed proposed income and that options are off the table that would increase income at this time, that the only way to balance the budget is to cut expenses. That's pretty elementary if you ask me. It's either that or simply make the election to go "PSYCHO." Again, remember the definition: "*seeming* to have difficulty distinguishing reality from fantasy,"

How do we cut spending when, like California and the U.S., we have already committed to all these expenditures and promised all these people that we were gonna provide payments and services? My answer is this - Eaasy!! No, I'm kidding – it's just that I, like many others, like the sound of that and wanted to hear somebody say it but it is really a pretty difficult task to undertake and requires making some fairly tough decisions. Let's lay all the cards on the table face up! Here are the options:

1. BANKRUPTCY
2. SELL THE CARS
3. VOLUNTARY REPOSESSION
4. SELL THE HOUSE
5. FORECLOSURE
6. REFINANCE HOME/ DEBT CONSOLIDATION

Different circumstances require different considerations and decisions, of course. Some people's only option is gonna be to file for chapter 7 or 13 bankruptcy relief because their situation is beyond repair. An example of this situation would be the guy who is leveraged to the hilt financially, i.e. he has no equity in his home or even worse owes more than it is worth; he is upside down in his automobiles; he has unsecured lines of credit and credit cards which are all maxed out, many of which are already charged off; his credit is shot; he is under threat of civil litigation by one or more creditors; his balance sheet is in the red; his expenses extend 20% or more beyond his current income. The guy in this situation though he means very well is probably sure to have to elect the chapter 7 bankruptcy option but only after seeking extensive legal and financial counsel. However be careful to seek COMPETENT counsel before making this decision.

Thank God that everybody's situation, as bad as it may seem, is not this extreme and can employ much less radical measures. Let's consider **Example B**. This guy has all of the above problems of the likely candidate for bankruptcy except that his credit score is still okay (around 640) and he has plenty of equity in his home. And by the way, this guy just lucked out and can take no credit for being in a better situation as he simply did not realize that he had the equity. If he had, he'd of surely taken out lines of credit and squandered that away too. While I have never been known to applaud ignorance, I am ecstatic that this guy was ignorant of his refinance options before now because it is the only reason along with his FICO score he has a feasible way out of this tragic situation.

This fellow has very good total household income to the tune of $75,000 per year and would easily qualify for refinancing his home to access all the $74,000 in equity that is available. His automobile is a 3 year old Infinity that he purchased used. He managed to obtain a pretty decent interest rate on it but is still upside down in it and still owes a total of $19,000. The car's fair market value is only about $12,000. The wife's vehicle is two year old Chevy Suburban in which $21,600 is owed. It's fair market value is only $18,000. They have a combined 13 credit cards (all maxed out) which total a whopping $21,000.00 and 4 other consumer loans that total $6,000.00. All these together flaunt a colossal total of $67,600.00.

This guy and his family would be prime candidates for refinancing their home by way of a debt consolidation loan. That is, only if they've gotten steps one through three resolved because we all know how the story will end if they had not. They would simply free up all of those credit cards and lines only to tap them again but this time finding themselves in the dreadful position of the first guy who has no other choice but to join the nation's bankruptcy statistics.

Anyway, this fellow was fortunate in that he purchased his home well under value at a time when the market was rapidly appreciating. He only owed $124,000 on his home with an $800.00 mortgage payment and a recent appraisal landed his home's fair market value at $198,000. This lucky fellow, though he was unaware of it, had the potential answer to much of his financial crisis literally in his own living room. The total of all of this family's monthly debt service to these loans including the $800.00 mortgage totaled an amazing $4,030.00. If they simply refinanced their home and tapped all of the 74,000 equity consolidating it all into one monthly mortgage, it would reduce the monthly payments from $4,030.00 to just $1,475. This frees up $2,170.00 a month so that now they have every dollar they need to subscribe to the recommended budget scale and begin building wealth.

In this case, no one had to go get a second job and no material possession had to be relinquished. Both of the vehicles are free and clear and all the credit cards and lines of credit boast zero balances. If only this family would adhere strictly to the 35% rule and maintain spending only the 65% and refuse to spend by credit, they will witness $15,000 in Cash savings in just 12 months - $7,500 in a short 6 months. While there are a couple of other recommendations I'd make, such as downsizing one of the newer vehicles and making extra principle payments on the mortgage, this family is rescued and on their way.

Now let's consider **Example C**. This is a horse of a different color. This family has a combined monthly income of only $2,900.00 yet has managed to obtain 9 credit cards totaling $14,000.00 with $600 total monthly payments to service them. They have two newer vehicles of course in which they owe a combined $36,000 with monthly payments totaling $850.00. Rent payments on the 3 bedroom 2 bath apartment that they live in runs $700.00 a month. My friends, this is a sad commentary.

Firstly, I will say that the one good thing this family had going for it was the fact that they had good credit but of course that is gone now. Good credit can be a curse and a blessing – blessing if you are financially literate and disciplined; a curse if you're ignorant concerning finances and not so disciplined (to put it nicely). In this case, this couple accepted every extension of credit offered without regards to a budget of any kind. They received flyers in the mail from the local car dealerships and bought the most expensive cars the banks would let them have. They would have gotten Mercedes Benzes if the bank had permitted. Then the credit card offers came pouring in so shoes, purses, stereos, rims and gold "teef" accented the fancy automobiles. They had jumped 2 classes in status all during a short period of about 6 months.

This couple of course is upside down in both automobiles as they were required to make only small down payments on them which didn't even cover the tax, title, and license fees. They are chronic renters and own no real estate at all that they could rely on to aid them in debt consolidation and their monthly expenses now exceed their modest monthly income. In fact, this couple has no intelligence whatsoever about the concept of homeownership and as they both came from families who were generations of renters. Renting is all they knew. They saw renting a nicer apartment outside of the projects as a major leap forward so you can imagine the excitement they experienced when discovering the advantages that their newfound credit scores provided. Again, it all boils down to lack of education.

This couple's case is truly typical of what many other couples in America – young and old- are facing today. The options are pretty limited and are as follows:

1. File bankruptcy.
2. Enroll in consumer credit counseling where a feasible payment plan is reached among all creditors.
3. Get a second job to make up the difference.
4. Jump off a bridge? Don't be stupid!!!

Again, I am not an attorney or financial advisor but here we have guys who are prime candidates for bankruptcy. Chapter 13 would basically force creditors into the position of reducing and restructuring their debt and monthly payments to affordable ones over a three (3) year period. However Chapter 7 would probably be the election that a bankruptcy attorney would most likely advise as it would literally wipe away all of the unsecured debt and allow the couple to reinstate the auto loans if they desired. The problem here though is that the autos are not worth the value of the debt and the couple cannot afford them anyway. If they are going the route of bankruptcy anyhow, especially Chapter 7, it would probably make more sense to turn the vehicles in and start all over again, only doing it right this time. What sense does it make to get a second chance and start right back out on the same path at a disadvantage by shelling out almost half your income in car notes?

I realize that my critics will complain that I am advocating that people shun their responsibilities and not do the best that they can to pay whatever portion they are able toward their debts, even in bankruptcy. Look, I didn't create the bankruptcy system nor the benefits and advantages it avails. My job is simply to make information available to those who find or put themselves in these terrible situations and offer lawful solutions that will enable them to recover and get back on the right track. I strongly discourage the willful misuse and abuse of this avenue although the wealthy have been proudly doing so for centuries.

Just like in the case of the 5th Amendment, it's perfectly okay for them along with their family and colleagues to benefit but once others such as the poor, middle-classed and otherwise ignorant discover and employ it, all of sudden foul play is decried. In some cases, attorneys and financial advisors alike will attempt to make a couple in this position feel guilty and give rotten advice contrary to conventional wisdom and inconsistent with what they'd do or have done themselves. The truth is that the rich benefit substantially more from the bankruptcy code than the poor could ever imagine to.

Enrolling in consumer credit counseling is an option that has worked for people in this situation. What happens here, in a nutshell, is an independent company (which much of the time is not so independent) comes in and mediates between the creditors and debtor with the goal of reaching satisfactory repayment arrangements. Many times they are successful in getting all or most of the debtor's payments reduced to affordable ones. They generally get interest rates abated, late fees eliminated and sometimes even settlements on principal amounts.

I must inform you, though, that it has been discovered that many of these consumer credit counseling services are set up, sponsored, and even owned by the very creditors that they are negotiating with. So debtor beware! Some advertise that they are not for profit organizations when in reality, they are. Therefore in dealing with them it would be wise to be advised of how, why, and who's sponsoring them? And just because an organization's status is Non-Profit doesn't mean that they don't receive payments or income. The reason corporations set up a lot of these credit counseling corporations is simply to have another vehicle by which they can collect their accounts receivable. We aren't supposed to be aware of this but what does it matter anyhow – if we create the debts, we should do what we can to make good on them. This is just FYI.

Getting a second job as the solution to financial chaos is rarely ever the answer. I say that because until a person deals with the first two directives that we discussed earlier in the chapter, getting a second job or more income only increases the resources that are available to consume. We have to understand that it's the Rat Race! It's the proverbial dog chasing his tail – although he may manage to pick up the pace and run faster, he's never gonna actually catch it. Therefore getting a second job only serves to make the 4th option of jumping off a bridge more appealing as life tends to get pretty frustrating once you add more work, time away from home, physical and mental anguish to an already dreadful scenario.

And as for suicide, life is too precious a gift to be reduced or compared to financial fulfillment. Every day that we are alive and privileged to breathe fresh air should be cherished and no matter how broke or financially challenged a person may be, the one thing that MAN hasn't been able to confine and offer for sale through the financial markets is the natural air we breathe. I am so thankful that we don't have to go down to the local city halls and buy air as we do electricity. I can't imagine what predicament we'd be in if we couldn't pay our AIR bills. And what about those of us who may have bad credit? We'd have to put our AIR in our cousin's name. You see folks, I'm thankful -and as long we have breath in our bodies and free air, despite our circumstances otherwise, we have life and hope. And at all costs, no matter what adversities or challenges we face, we must always labor to live and – as the Rev. Jesse Jackson preaches – "Keep hope alive!"

Finally, we will deal with **Example D**. This family is in pretty bad shape financially as the previous. They have a combined household income of $25,000.00 annually. They own their own home which is valued at about $85,000.00 and owe approximately $80,000.00 on it. They have low FICO scores in range of the mid 550's and are servicing a mortgage with a payment of $725.00 per month. This couple only has one automobile loan financed at a 22% interest rate at a local finance company. Their payments are $455.00 a month on a 5 year old Ford Expedition – they have a separate stereo and chrome wheels payment of $125.00 to go with it.

The truck is "clean" though! The goods news is that they only have about 6 more months before both the Expedition and the accessories are paid off. Between 5 high interest credit cards, they've managed to run up over $12,000.00 in revolving debt and pay a whopping $475.00 a month to service them. All of them are maxed out, of course, with 2 over the limit and because they do not pay them on time, each month the balances are steadily climbing as the credit card companies tack on their notorious over the limit and late fees – to the tune of $29.00 apiece.

This family is not really in enough debt to merit filing bankruptcy although people in their situation do it with less everyday. While I do admit that they are still in way over their heads, they actually have options that will result in their vindication if they are willing to put in the sweat. Let's explore some them.

1. Acknowledge their financial behavior as psychotic and commit to changing their mindset and practices.
2. Create a sound budget.
3. Enroll in Consumer Credit Counseling.
4. Get a second job to make up the difference.
5. Employ the 35% Rule.

Now I am tenaciously against second and third jobs for the reason I explained previously but they can be effective solutions temporarily for some cases. In this case, where the income to expenses gap is close enough and considering the fact that they'd be eliminating the $475.00 and $125.00 monthly payments in 6 months, it is too tempting not to buckle down and make a 6 month run for it. Assuming that a counseling company will accept them (not all cases will qualify) and can reduce their monthly credit card payments by about 40 to 50%, there is light at the end of the tunnel for these guys. This dude can get a second job or hustle on the side and make an extra $400.00 a month for the next 6 months and free up that extra $600.00 bucks which should go toward savings and retiring the credit card debt. And don't forget the application of the first 35% rule!

In considering these four cases, we find that all have the same fundamental deficiencies and can be summarized in two areas.

1. Failure to operate by the 35% rule. Takes care of the consumer problem.

2. Not operating on a sound budget.

It doesn't matter how much or how little income we generate, we have to come to grips with the fact that we cannot spend all or more than we make. This seems so very simple to grasp yet it is so hard to make reality in our lives because we have experienced just the opposite for so long. We cannot spend every dime that comes into our hands. We have to keep saying it over and over again and even write it down a hundred times like when we were kids in school in an earnest attempt to try to reprogram our destructive thinking. It is psychotic both to engage in spending or consuming everything that comes into our hands and likewise to not on purpose save and invest a portion of it in the process. It is "disordered, demented, crazy, loony," and outright "nuts!"

Attaining financial independence, I've found, is not rocket science. It's really pretty elementary and would happen almost mechanically if we would simply apply the principles laid out in this chapter. If everybody would embrace this concept concerning finances, almost no one would be poor or without ample resources. Our problem is that we have become ingrained Consumers. It is a state of mind – the fruits resulting are merely the consequences of subscribing to such irrational behavior.

In conclusion, I would like to submit once again my simple formula that anyone can use that would put them on autopilot on the journey to attaining financial independence. In following these principles it would be virtually impossible to be broke ever again regardless of income or job status. And remember, even if one would merely adhere to just the first two principles they'd still end up a millionaire by retirement. It's a no brainer! For Pete's sake, if we are so stubborn to reject these principles by continuing with our irrational behavior, we should at least love our children enough to want to see them delivered. Certainly we should at the very least want to give them the fighting chance many of us never had due to financial ignorance.

FINANCIAL GUIDELINES

1. Allocates Religiously The First 35% Of Gross Income as follows:

A.	Tithes/Gifts	10%
B.	Long Term Savings	10%
C.	Short Term Savings	10%
D.	Household Savings	3%
E.	Emergency	2%

2. Allocates Remaining 65% As follows:

   A. FICA Taxes   7.65%

       Federal & State Taxes   Varies By Bracket

   B. Mortgage (P&I, Ins./Taxes)   24%

   C. Transportation (Pays cash for cars)   0%

   D. Utilities, Food, Insurances,   33%

   E. Entertainment, Clothing, Etc.

3. Pays Credit Card Balances In Full Monthly.

4. Always pays bills on time.

5. Owns primary home and rental property as well.

6. Purposely Maintains a 740 or above FICO score.

CHAPTER 7

UNDERSTANDING THE POWER OF A 700 FICO OR BEACON SCORE!

This chapter may prove to be the most important chapter in the book if you were ignorant like me. It will literally change lives if it is embraced objectively and applied as directed. It should be a required read for every student from grade school through college.

As African Americans we just do not realize the tool we have in the credit scoring system of America. It is truly fascinating and we don't seem to understand its significance. Beacon and FICO scores to me are up there in importance with things like FREEDOM and the right to VOTE! But we are ignorant of their power. I advocate that we need to protect our personal credit just like it was one of our children. We'd never put our kids in harm's way nor do anything that would knowingly harm them. We stick up for them through thick and thin building them up, nurturing and carefully examining and monitoring them all their lives until they are able to care for themselves. I submit to all that we need to treat our personal credit with similar love, care, and respect. I'm serious!

With banking becoming so driven by technology we find that nowadays everything is pretty much automated and that credit has reduced for the most part to a numbers game. Everything from home loans to auto loans to major credit card loans and interest rates related thereto are all determined by this magic number that is called a Beacon or FICO score. We have all learned that if we maintain a 700 or above credit score, things tend to be significantly better for us financially. I would even go so far as to say many times it serves as a barrier breaker when it comes to African Americans and lending institutions.

It is great for us that we can apply and shop for Home Mortgage loans online with financial institutions and obtain approvals via automated systems opposed to individual bankers. This is a gift from heaven. Traditionally we were somewhat disadvantaged in that we had to visit personally a banker at a local branch for these types of loans and sweat bullets hoping and praying that he would think enough of us to grant us a loan, regardless of how good our credit was. And we've already learned that probably 97% of bankers who have decision making power in America are White. It's not as much their fault that those percentages are that high as it is ours. Nonetheless it is what it is. Much of the prejudices that occurred in times past has been eradicated on the personal side of banking when the automated systems were established. Now it's a different story altogether when it comes down to business banking but we will not address that in this chapter.

With automated scoring systems dominating the industry, it has almost turned Black people into Whites when it comes down to obtaining premier mortgage loans at prime interest rates. It is a documented fact that White mortgage bankers (not so long ago) discriminated rampantly against Black qualified applicants because of their race. What's more it is also widely known that bankers purposely charged Black applicants significantly higher interest rates than they did White applicants with the same credit profiles. Federal government agencies were actually found to be guilty of these practices and even settled tons of lawsuits for these practices.

I am personally aware of this as I remember my Aunt Matt explaining to us how her and her husband would go and apply for government farm loans and were outright denied because they were too dark in complexion. They noticed in the process, however, that their colleagues and neighbors who were White farmers in the same community would be granted the loans with ease despite the fact that they were less qualified. Needless to say, my Aunt and her husband along with numbers of Black farmers ended up losing their farms and equipment due to lack of funding. Nevertheless, the government settled with my Aunt after years of struggle and financial hardship for a substantial amount of money – upper six figures. So for all the skeptics who swear this doesn't or hasn't happened, here is strict proof thereof.

So you see, I love this invisible system that doesn't prejudge an applicant by the color of his skin or by the clothes he is wearing because it can't see them over the computer screen. All it sees is a credit profile which is largely made up of a FICO score – then if figures in debt to income ratio, and assets possessed.

This automated banking system is prophecy fulfilled and Dr. Martin Luther King, Jr.'s dream partially realized. I understand that Dr. King dreamed that White people would personally judge us by the content of our character and not just a mere computer model but hey, close enough for the time being. There are still some loop holes with this system with regard to zip code profiling but for the most part it has opened up a whole new level of opportunity where personal credit is concerned.

Once again ignorance has a tendency to rob us of any benefits, in roads, and advantages gained by this FICO system and many others. Therefore it is so vitally important that we endeavor to understand and appreciate the value of these vehicles and take full advantage of them. While many African Americans are complaining about the disparities that exist (and they do) in this country and demanding that the government take more measures to close gaps even further (and it should), we find that Blacks are not embracing the systems that are already in place to make up the hedges.

I often wondered why the nation's school systems do not teach students about topics such as personal finance and credit. It seems to me that these issues are so vitally important that certainly our school boards and educational administrators are bright enough to know that our children are doomed to financial failure without this knowledge. I just don't understand it. But instead of complaining about the obvious, the prudent thing to do is for us to take the initiative independently to become financially literate and likewise make certain that our children receive the same.

I've never had the privilege of attending private schools so I cannot say whether their curriculum allows for it but it just seems to me that it is so irresponsible of our school systems public or private to send our nation's children in the world so ill-prepared to succeed financially. I am a strong advocate for a good education but what I want to know is: "If Jimmy left for San Francisco from San Antonio by bicycle at 2:00 PM on Thursday and George left from the same place by car at 8:00

A.M. 2 days later, who will arrive in San Francisco first and at what time?" What does that have to do with real life and being successful therein?

Now I realize that those trivial essay questions have some significance like when planning a mission to outer space or something and that's great. However, before you get into to all that, teach our children how to create a sound budget, the importance of sticking to it, the significance of establishing and maintaining great credit, and saving or investing for the future. After all, the power of compounding interest is a principle that can be taught to 5th graders. Come on, we can't be competitive with other nations when the vast majority of our population are proud "CONSUMERS" of everything we get our hands on and financially illiterate.

This is an indictment on our country's Educational System and leaders but a call to action for every parent wants their children to be the best they can be and live their lives to the fullest. For those of us who are poor or otherwise financially challenged because of our ignorance, it would be a disgrace to allow our kids to experience the heartache and agony that we subjected ourselves to because we did not appreciate or value the gift and power of a great credit score.

The thing about the credit FICO system is that absolutely everyone can and should have a credit score of over 700. Many believe that a 740 or higher credit score can only be obtained by the White people in great authority like Senators and diplomats or the affluent. This couldn't be any further from the truth. The truth is that even the poorest guy in the city who works for minimum wage at the local convenient store can and should have a high credit score. Some of us believe that credit agencies hand these scores out as they choose, giving high scores to the rich White folks and all the brothers get the crumbs – you know, the 450's and 500's. Again, a lot of us Blacks and Whites alike are ignorant of the FICO system and how it works thus resulting in many of us esteeming its importance very little.

A good or bad FICO score has nothing to do with where a person works or how much money they make. It has nothing whatsoever to do with a person's race, religion, creed, or social status. I have seen politicians, preachers, White folks, Black folks, little sweet old ladies, professors, as well as accountants all with jacked up credit scores in the low to mid 400's.

Being an automobile salesman in my younger days, I would be responsible for gathering personal information and pulling a customer's FICO score to determine credit worthiness. Boy, boy, boy! It's one thing to have jacked up credit – it's another to have jacked up credit and perpetrate the fraud by getting a poor sales person's (trying to earn a decent living and take care of his wife and 5 children) hopes up knowing good and well that they hadn't paid their Momma back, let alone a creditor.

These guys were always the ones that worked you down to the bone on price -$100.00 Flat Commission- and stayed at the dealership for hours tying up a brother's whole day. "By the way, how's your credit Mr. Councilman?" I'd ask. Or my favorite, "On a scale of 1 to 10, with 10 being the highest, how would you rate your credit?" They'd often reply, "Oh credit's good, young man!" So you know I get all excited and take the application to the manager and pace the floor waiting for the verdict. Much of the time these high classed people that you would expect would have the 740 FICO scores couldn't buy a box of Cracker Jacks on credit. They couldn't get a bank to loan them $20.00 even with a co-signer. I remember my manager telling me one night to, "Chase that guy out my showroom! Git, git, git em outta here!"

I don't mean to belittle or make fun of people in this predicament but only to emphasize the point that all types of people have messed up credit. The very people you would swear had perfect credit you'd be amazed to discover that they are in similar straits and even worse.

Then on the other hand, I have witnessed customers that come in who I knew lived in a single wide trailer in the local trailer park, but with perfect credit – all aces, as I called it! That's what's up! This lady didn't make much money either. I may not have been able to make a huge commission because her income was limited, but I knew she would get approved for a loan so a brother was guaranteed to get the sale and a commission of some kind. Can you dig it? Somehow this lady, who was Black by the way, managed to learn and put in to practice sound principles of finance and appreciated the power of maintaining outstanding credit. I shall never forget that lady and the lesson she taught everybody at the dealership that day about prejudging people.

Credit scores and profiles are determined by each individual's repayment practices. It's up to each person what his or her score is gonna be and their financial behavior determines it. The system has a reputation of being very ambiguous and complex but is actually quite simple and as we begin to understand how it grades us we can begin to configure on purpose the credit profile and score that we desire.

Most people are either really good with their finances or really terrible but in neither case do many actually understand how they got the score they have - only that they pay all their bills on time or pay none of them on time. Actually, a person could pay all of their bills on time faithfully every month but still have a low credit score and not qualify for a mortgage or auto loan. Then on the other hand, a person could actually pay all of his bills 29 days late every month and have a 700 credit score and qualify for basically whatever he wants. This is what frustrates so many people and explains why they feel that this credit score business is largely unfair. Once we understand how the system grades us, it'll make perfect sense. There's no need to continue to grumble and complain about something that is never gonna change to accommodate us – the smart thing to do is stop letting the system work us but become educated on what makes it tick, and begin to work the system to our advantage.

I love the FICO scoring system and it's simply because I understand it. I don't hope, wish, pray, or beg the system to deal favorable with me as most Americans do. Neither am I on pins and needles when I go to apply for a loan of some type wondering if the banker is gonna approve my application. I know exactly where I stand before I attempt to secure business financing on a piece of real estate for two reasons. Number one is I don't want to look like a moron or feel like an idiot when I'm sitting across from the business banker who is looking at my credit on his computer screen. I'm gonna know exactly what he's looking at and not with my fingers and toes crossed hoping that somehow everything or at least "something" on the report looks okay.

And the second reason is I always make sure that I am empowered with the information that is necessary to ensure that I am speaking to him from a position of strength whereby I can negotiate favorable financing terms. Most people, especially those of us who may have credit challenges, deal from a "I hope I get approved" position where it is evident to the bankers or managers that we're ignorant of the system. As a result we are then prone, more specifically at car dealerships, to be charged higher rates even though we may have great credit scores. Ignorance, financially or otherwise, is not a virtue!

I want to take this time to offer 5 reasons why everyone should put a demand of themselves to establish and maintain great credit scores. As I stated before, our credit should be highly regarded and prioritized way up there with stuff like . . . yeah, our Kids!

5 Reasons To Have Good Credit And High Credit Scores

1. High credit scores can qualify us for the best interest rates and terms on loans which means we pay less.

2. High credit scores portray us to others as responsible and trustworthy in not just financial matters, but as a whole.

3. High credit scores put us in a better position to realize our dreams such as nice homes and leverage for investing.

4. High credit scores can be the determining factor of whether or not we are hired for certain employment positions. Employers now are reviewing credit as part of their employee interviewing and screening processes.

5. High credit scores are qualifiers when choosing spouses. A high credit score just might be the thing that tips the scale in your favor when your potential spouse is weighing whether she'll say "I do" or "I'd better not."

5 REASONS TO NOT HAVE LOW SCORES AND BAD CREDIT

1. Consumers with bad credit pay more for everything they buy on credit to the tune of double and sometimes triple in some cases. The prime interest rate on a 30 year mortgage right now is about 5.9%. Consumers with bad credit can expect to pay 10 to 12%. A good credit consumer would pay about $593.14 on a $100,000.00 mortgage whereas a bad credit consumer would pay about $877.57. A good credit consumer would pay interest of about 7% on credit card accounts where his counterpart would pay 29%. The same is true for automobile loans. The average rate on a new car for good credit buyers is about 5% and up to 18% or more for those with bad credit.

2. Consumers with bad credit are generally viewed as untrustworthy, financially illiterate, and irresponsible in not just money matters but everything else as well.

3. Consumers with bad credit are often denied the ability to attain their goals in life due to their wreckless records. Employers now look at credit reports to help determine the overall character of applicants prior to hiring. How can a person be responsible for making key financial decisions with a corporation when they've established by their credit file that

they've made a mess of their own personal finances. This is an eye-opening reality and many employers don't even disclose that they are reviewing your credit. But read the disclosure at the bottom of their employment applications that you are required to sign. This may be the reason you didn't get that job that you just knew you'd get.

4. Consumers with bad credit disqualify themselves from rental or lease opportunities because of poor credit histories. Many apartment agencies luxury and otherwise will not rent to applicants with scores below certain levels.

5. Consumers with bad credit can be eliminated from becoming on the short list of the best choices in life-companions because their credit history indicates that they are irresponsible and have a proven track record of making poor choices.

Now I fully realize that these are some pretty tough pills to swallow and really don't require a lot of elaboration but I thought it fitting to supplement just a little where the adverse credit was concerned.

Having experienced the devastating effects and compensation of low FICO scores and bad credit, I feel I can openly talk to those of us who find ourselves in this predicament currently. Believe me, I feel your pain and know what it's like personally to be in such a position. It's like a self inflicted sentence to slavery all over again and to those who have never been enslaved or second classed citizens, having bad credit gets you as close as you can get. If for no other reason, everybody should strive to get out of this situation because of this reality alone.

Having bad credit gives creditors license to treat people with lack of respect and dishonor. It empowers bill collectors to talk to grown men and women like they are children and interrogate them profusely during the process when many of those doing the bill collecting are in similar or worse positions. Nonetheless, the recipients of this degradation are in no position to resist for fear of adverse action being taken resulting in repossession, foreclosure, or lawsuit.

I remember getting mad and copping an attitude with bill collectors when they called all times of the day and night. Each time it seemed that they were all taking my deposition individually and it angered me to be treated like that. However, I had no choice but to concede that I put myself in that position. I had to acknowledge the fact that if I had only sent them their money when I agreed to they wouldn't be calling. They weren't calling just for kicks – they were trying to get the money they were owed and because of it, I had to be subject to them. A wise man said, " The rich rule over the poor and the borrower is servant to the lender." I know that's right! Well if that is so, why do we knowingly and so eagerly sign up to be indentured servants? Makes no sense does it? We have to transform our thinking.

Who came up with this ridiculous mindset anyway? It is psychotic! We even go so far as to go in debt for sneakers and pocket books and high heel shoes – gold rims and gold teeth. We sign up as servants for riding lawn mowers, gas grills, furniture and stereos. This is insane when you really think about it.

I want to point out 8 things that I think are vitally important for everyone to know about their personal credit scores.

1. There are three major credit bureau agencies that lenders rely upon to examine the credit worthiness of applicants. They are Equifax, Experian, and Transunion.

2. More than 90% of people have errors of some kind that adversely affect their credit scores. Incorrect information can be disputed and corrected if one can demonstrate that the information is inaccurate.

3. Creditors are not allowed to report late payments made on a person's credit cards, mortgages, installment loans and other reported accounts until they are OVER 30 days late. A person could actually pay every credit card or installment account 29

days late every single month for 20 years and maintain a 740 Fico score though it would be ill-advised.

4. Accounts such as utilities, cable, internet, home and cell Phones are generally not reported monthly on personal credit reports. They are, however, reported as derogatory once they become over 30 days delinquent, are turned over to collections, or are charged off.

5. Rent payment history is not reported on personal credit reports. However judgements due to unpaid rent can be reported.

6. Using over 35% of available credit on credit cards can adversely affect a personal credit score by 100 points or more depending on the number of credit cards in this state and various balance to availability ratios. *This explains why a consumer can pay every account on time each month but still have a score in the 500's – they are simply maxed out and the scoring systems reflects it.*

7. Inquiries on a personal credit report are crucial. Every time a person applies for credit and their credit is pulled, that inquiry is reflected on the person's credit report and lowers their score. Be careful to limit these inquiries. Be aware that car dealerships and some online mortgage and credit card companies will send your information to 10 or more lenders at a time seeking approval and it could kill your score. And also be aware that now a days companies are pulling all three bureaus.

8. Check your credit often – every other month at least. Identity theft is one of the fastest growing crimes in the world where criminals are stealing the identity of consumers and opening new credit accounts in their names. These accounts go unpaid of course and can totally destroy a person's credit profile. It generally takes an act of congress to dispute and correct it when it occurs. Vigilance is the key as it is commonly reported that consumers are the victims of identity theft months before they know it because they do not monitor their credit.

CHAPTER 8

FOUR

METHODS OF

PRODUCING

MONEY!

This is probably gonna be the most interesting portion of the book for many of us simply because no matter how rich or how poor a person may be, somehow the ability to be able to earn a decent or good income is a vital part of the American Dream - and rightly so. I realize that talking plainly about making money seems very base to some because we've been taught that money isn't everything and is really not that important. While I agree that money isn't everything, I also agree with King Solomon when he said, "money answereth all things." Money cannot buy all things but it can buy most things and is very important to have in the society in which we live. Moreover, our intelligence concerning making money, keeping money, and handling money has a major impact on our happiness. You ain't gotta say, "Amen," but it's true anyhow.

The people that say that money doesn't make you feel good hasn't had any because you do feel better when you've got some versus when you have none. We're healthier and happier when we can pay the mortgage on time and don't have to be stressing about where the money's coming from. We feel great when we can buy groceries and provide for our children and pay for them to have the very best education. I don't know about you but that "feels" good to me and I understand that it takes more than money to have JOY but I've also come to realize that money along with JOY is a beautiful thing.

Poor people are quick to boast that they have JOY as if to suggest that JOY and money somehow isn't a perfect fit. I submit to you that it is and we need to work at learning better and more efficient ways to earn money and more of it. The better we become at this, we'll undoubtedly find that the better our quality of lives will ultimately become. Money may not be everything and it may not bring JOY but neither does being broke, working 12 hour days and two and three jobs – and not being able to spend quality time with our families.

With the constant downsizing of corporate America and strategic outsourcing of jobs to foreign nations, we can no longer depend upon the advice and mindset so firmly instilled in all of us by our parents, teachers, and mentors. We were taught from the time we were in kindergarten that we were to study hard, get a good education which included high school and college (maybe even law or medical school) and get a good job. We are finding out more and more everyday as we live in the 21st century that this is a flawed mentality and not nearly as reliable as it once was. We find ourselves still living by the prevalent concepts that reigned for much of the 80's and early 90's but are proven at the very least much less effective in the times that we now live in.

The truth is that in this technological age the expectation of landing a high paying corporate level job, working for 30 years and retiring with a nice pension is not something that we can hang our hats on anymore. I apologize but it is just not realistic in the world that we live in today. The days of depending upon corporate giants as IBM, AT&T and others is a thing of the past and whether we want to openly admit or not, most of us know of certainty that I am exactly right. And it used to be that the blue collar workers were safe and could always depend upon companies like GM and Ford Motor Company. After all, it made plenty of sense that automobiles weren't going any place so there would always be jobs there. The closing of many Ford Plants right in our backyards were sobering eye openers of just how drastic our economy and world has changed as it relates to how companies do business.

I have heard stories of co-workers going to work after 20 years on the job with their fingers crossed and afraid to check their mail boxes for fear of discovering a pink slip therein. How does a grown man deal with that being 45 years old and having committed to a company all those years only to realize he was just a number and all of a sudden has to start all over? What does he tell his wife and children at home? I have heard of instances where grown men after receiving their lay-off notices at work fall to their knees and weep in despair not even caring that their coworkers are watching because their world was now shattered. And those who witnessed these occurrences knew that the next day or month that that could very well be there own reality.

Corporate America has changed dramatically, no doubt but our philosophies have not done so at the rate of the industries that we serve. And we do our children a disservice by not quickly adapting and educating them in what we see happening right before our very eyes. It seems that we are in a daze – in denial even. Snap out of it America! Things are not going back to the way they were and simply "a hoping and a wishin and a prayin" is not gonna change that – I'm sorry! We are pretending that the inevitable is not at hand. Just because we don't have any easy answers doesn't justify delaying action and acknowledgement of our dilemma. We don't know what to do ourselves and therefore are at an even more loss for words of advice for our children - other than the false hope of conventional wisdom that we've been preaching to them for the past 15 to 20 years.

We need to be honest with ourselves first and accept the fact that we cannot depend on companies to provide us with "good jobs" and pensions. This is not a sound financial strategy. When our employers are constantly offering us attractive early retirement packages, we have the audacity to brag about it as if we do not understand that what they are actually doing is trying to FIRE us! Come on, Homes! Read between the lines – they call themselves attempting to be cordial with us in hopes that we will take a hint and bow out gracefully. When fortune 500 companies, banks, and manufacturing companies offer us these sweet deals, they are really saying "Get your hat and coat – it's time to move on." But we won't go! Some of us really don't get it. This is not meant to be taken as a compliment.

Many, after having read this chapter are gonna wake up and realize for the first time that they have been being prepped for firing for months now and didn't have a clue about it. For those of us who still don't get it, let me deliver you and tell you what your friends, family members, and executives on the job are afraid to tell you - <u>THEY ARE TRYING TO FIRE YOU!</u>

Many of us are well aware of these realities and are not delusional as the previous example but are just as bad off because we won't take appropriate action now to lighten the blow. We know we are gonna crash or run off the cliff shortly and we have "some" time but we won't pump the brakes, look for a detour, nor even brace for impact. I say at least let the passenger on the other side know what's going on so they can make an intelligent decision about their own financial demise – let's at least let our children know what's up ahead. Remember all they know about what is up there is what we've been constantly telling them for the past 10 to 15 years which has proven to be false.

Conditions have drastically changed. There is danger ahead! Let's not be so full of pride that we cannot admit that we misjudged and that we now have to rethink things and perhaps abandon altogether the plan that we devised previously. I mean, we do love our children don't we? Certainly we wouldn't knowingly lead them down a wrong path or fail to avert actions and mindsets that we know will more than likely lead to financial disappointment and ruin. We have to level with them and tell them the truth.

Have we stopped to consider that while salaries are indexed to increase by a mere 3% per year, inflation is more than double that amount? Gas, food, and utilities are rising by double digits. We're on a tread mill here Guys and somebody keeps turning up the speed, and we just can't manage to keep up.

It goes without saying that this 21st century dilemma that we face regarding the job market is not limited or respective to African Americans. Therefore we are not speaking here of a Black or White issue but an American one – it's pure economics. So Blacks cannot claim as an excuse that the markets or industries have changed on us because the reality is that they have changed on everyone alike. In fact, Whites with the better classed and higher paying jobs are hit harder as you know the old saying, "the higher you are, the greater your fall." What do those high level executives earning $250,000.00 per year or more do when suddenly the rug is pulled out from under them after working their way to the top for 10 to 20 years? Yeah, I know they made a lot of money and you'd think they'd have some put away but they are just like everyone else consuming it at the same rate they were earning. Therefore with a $5,000.00 mortgage and hefty automobile payments in addition to country club membership, they've seen a bad day.

The key to it all, I'm convinced, is financial literacy. We have to understand money and finances and how they work. It is important that we explore the different methods of producing income. Throughout the years and our generations, we have only been taught one of those methods and it just so happens that it is least efficient of them all. But hey, it's all that many of us have ever known.

There are four (4) fundamental methods of producing income that I want to address – **Linear Income**, **Residual Income**, **Passive Income,** and **Portfolio Income**. I submit to everyone under the sound of my voice that we should be educated on and understand these concepts prior to setting goals and making final decisions about what areas of study and professions to embark upon. While I do agree that we should follow our passions and do what we love, I also believe that once we first come to understand the power of these principles and begin to plug in various professions to discover which categories they fall in, we may find that we will grow to love something else. Or at the very least we may decide to earn income totally separate from our life's passion. It may be that this strategic decision will enable us to do that work more effectively and on a much greater scale as a result. A lot of times we assume that the two are automatically entwined only to learn that many times doing our life's passion doesn't pay the bills very well. See how deranged our thinking can be? We've only been taught one way.

Let's look at **Linear Income**. The concept of earning Linear Income is our favorite – in fact it's the only one that we know and were taught. Linear Income is income that is generated by performing a given task once and getting paid for it once. That is the contract – that is the arrangement – that's the deal and everybody understands and agrees to it. On a regular job, we work for an hour and get paid for the hour that we worked. If we work 8 hours, that's what we expect to get paid for – no more, no less.

A perceived value is attributed by both sides to the work that is performed and regardless of the future benefit or appreciation in value of that work to the employer, the employee basically settles in full for the wage paid. The employer on the other hand gets the immediate benefit of the work performed along with the expectation that the work will ultimately yield increase beyond just that moment it was enacted.

With Linear Income, the recipient thereof is almost guaranteed to always get the short end of the stick. And they are supposed to. Everybody knows that the investor or the guy or company that's taking all the risk should be the recipient of the greatest reward. It's a fundamental principle that is accepted by all – it's a given. Nobody argues with that as it is only right.

A great employee who is a customer service representative or concierge at a Five Star hotel in metro Atlanta is very professional and personable in her interaction with elite guests. Patrons are charged a hefty $400.00 per night for accommodations. The concierge gets paid a decent $12.00 an hour to meet, greet, and serve the needs of their guests daily. She is so personable that the patrons of the hotel choose to come back to the hotel over and over again because of her and also refer other business colleagues who also begin to frequent the hotel. They go on to have annual banquets and meetings there as well all because of the impeccable service rendered by this concierge. It has literally translated into millions of dollars in additional business over a short 2 year period as repeat and referral business had snow balled.

This is fantastic for the hotel but catastrophic for the concierge even though she does not know it. The concierge is very content with her wages and doesn't appear to even notice the effect she is having financially on the hotel's bottom line. All she knows is that she signed up for $12.00 an hour or Linear Income and that the hotel has kept its end of the bargain for the past two years. She is well aware that she is doing a fantastic job and as a result she was properly rewarded by receiving a dollar an hour raise twice - for that she was grateful. She worked an hour and got paid an agreed upon amount for each hour of work performed.

The concierge got her pay and the hotel received the benefit for the work performed and kept all the value left over. When the concierge clocked out each day, her expectation of pay ceased yet the hotel's cash register was still ringing because of the work she performed. In fact, the concierge could quit or get fired and chances are the hotel would still benefit for years to come off of the referrals and repeat business that she generated. This is the problem with producing Linear Income. A valued employee performs a task once and can only hope to receive pay for it once despite the fact that the employer will get paid over and over for that task.

The flawed concept of working for Linear Income doesn't really hit home until we consider the fact that our gas bill runs 24 hours a day. It doesn't dawn on us until we consider the fact that we stop working at 5pm but our bills run around the clock. You see we didn't even realize how much trouble we were actually in before now. When we look at it from this prospective, we realize that somehow someway we have got to figure out how to make money while we're asleep, just to keep up with the bills!

Now let's take a look at **RESIDUAL INCOME**. Just the term alone sounds like it's better than Linear Income. Residual income is a concept that poor people often go through life and never even hear about, let alone partake or be trained in. It is the wealthy man's best kept secret and the very key to establishing empires and financial dominance. It is absolutely appalling to me and should be to you as well that this fundamental wealth principle is not taught in school – and I mean elementary school as well as high school.

The concept of earning residual income is simply performing a task once and getting paid for it over and over again. This principle is so elementary yet so foreign to 95% of Americans. That's why only 5% of the nation's population have 80% of the nation's wealth. The 5% are the wealthy and they all operate proficiently in this simple principle and they do it on purpose. Many of us, on the other hand are totally ignorant of what's going on and even when opportunities are presented to us which involve residual income, we run from them as the concepts are so alien to us. We turn down flat opportunities to get involved with producing residual and passive income but will swim across oceans for a job opportunity. This is pitiful!

I have heard many refer to these opportunities as too good to be true while at the same time we see our employers and the affluent reap the benefits of them every single day. We witness the results of residual income every time we go to work and many of us regularly create it for our bosses on a daily basis. The sad part of it all is that we don't even understand the magnitude of what an amazing vehicle we are creating. So naturally it is highly unlikely that we would ever think to create any of it for ourselves or even figure out a way to get paid for it beyond just the present. All we know is we work an hour and get paid for that hour we worked without giving any thought whatsoever whether or not that hour worked pays our employer a dividend beyond what was evident.

Again, ignorance is not a virtue but employers appreciate it in their employees. They laugh as we are on pins and needles when trying to muster up the nerve to ask them for a dollar an hour raise. They marvel at how ignorant many employees are concerning their true value to the company. It amazes them in discovering how eager workers are to labor so diligently for "peanuts" not being intelligent enough to even inquire about residuals for their work.

A good example of residual income is an independent insurance agent who goes out and lands a modest insurance policy on a potential client. He takes the time to drive out to the client's home to meet him and his wife. They agree to a 10 year $50,000.00 whole life policy where the annual premium is $1,900.00. The agent spends about 2 hours with the client and writes the policy collecting the first monthly premium payment in advance of $158.34. The agent's payable commission on the policy is $475.00 a year or $39.58 per month as this client has elected to pay in installments.

Therefore the insurance agent in this case is in the business of creating residual income by performing a task once but getting paid for it over and over again. He performed a 2 hour task and will get paid $475.00 a year for the next 10 years never having to even speak to that client again. That is, until it is time to renew at such time as he'll simply put the process in motion all over again.

Let's do the mathematics here. If this insurance agent wants to earn $75,000.00 per year which is about the average salary of the average corporate level employee, he would only need to acquire 158 or so clients who would agree to purchase a similar 10 year $50,000.00 whole life insurance policy. The math is simple: Just take $75,000.00 (desired earnings) and divide it by the annual commission paid per client ($475.00).

So let's get this straight. The corporate worker is trained to go to college, get a 4 year degree in business, go on to get his masters, and get a good job in corporate America. He'll probably start out with $65,000.00 and in about 5 years hit the glass ceiling of $75,000.00 and hope they will keep him on for the next 30 years and he can afford to retire. Mind you he has no real job security whatsoever and can be laid off or replaced at the drop of a hat. He is stressed everyday with deadlines to meet and works 10 hour days to meet them. The corporation tells him when he can go on vacation, how long he and his family can stay, and even tells him *how many days he can be sick each year*. He has to beg his boss to allow him to attend his child's school programs and is very rarely able to make it to his son's little league baseball games. Wait a minute – are we talking about a grown man here? You mean this guy creates residual income for the corporation but has personally agreed to accept a month's pay for a month's labor and has to ask his boss if he can go to his daughter's dance recital? Really?

The insurance agent, however, does not have a college degree nor does he boast a masters. Yet he simply sets out to land 158 clients that he can convince to purchase a measly 10 year $50,000.00 whole life policy (which I oppose because they are overpriced and a poor value) in a year's time. To accomplish this, all the agent has to do is land 13 clients under these circumstances per month (158 clients divided by 12mos) and he has just created a $75,000.00 annual income that is residual for the next 10 years. Once this is accomplished, he doesn't have to meet a schedule everyday at work. He doesn't have the stress of meeting all those unrealistic deadlines. He can go on vacation with his family whenever he wants and stay gone as long as he can afford to. And, oh, he has the liberty to be sick (although I strongly discourage this aspiration) as many days out of the year as he pleases. He can proudly be apart of his kids' first day of school and other programs, and make all the little league games. He can do this for the next 10 years as his income is absolute and virtually recession proof. This sounds like a fairy tale doesn't it? Almost even too good to be true – but we all are beginning to get the picture now.

The moral of the story is this - although the insurance agent was uneducated in society's opinion, he understood the valuable concept of residual income. He was financially literate when the corporate guy was just the opposite. He was well educated by all accounts and highly esteemed as a great intellectual but financial ignorance caused him to subscribe to the wrong method of long term income production. The uneducated insurance agent's motto was this, "Don't know much about history; don't know much biology – but I do have better since than to practice trading time for dollars or producing Linear Income."

Of course I am in no way suggesting that anyone who works for a corporation is an idiot. My point is that if they were better informed about the four income producing methods, they might decide that it would be more beneficial to choose more efficient means of earning income. Or, after being educated in these fundamental principles they may decide to take the income they earn from the linear method and invest in residual or passive vehicles.

So once again for the skeptics and critics, I am in no way advocating against a formal education. I am all for it. And I am in no wise teaching against working a corporate job although I am against relying heavily on it alone as a person's only plan for financial independence. It can certainly serve as a tool that will enable one to tap into the latter two. Besides, what are we gonna do with these degrees, throw them away? Absolutely not. We simply need to change the way we look at income production and wealth building and train our children accordingly.

Next, we have **Passive Income**. Much like residual income, passive income is a much smarter way to produce income and more efficient than linear. The IRS defines passive income as any activity that a person or entity produces in which the tax payer does not materially participate. Another definition is, "income derived from real estate and business investments in which the individual is not actively involved." In short, it's simply *getting paid for what someone else does*. Isn't that phenomenal? In this case, it's not necessarily our business - more often than not it is someone else's which means they do all the hard work, manage the overhead and employees and we just get paid every month. Passive income does not include earnings from wages or active business participation.

Wait a minute! That doesn't seem fair. It almost sounds too good to be true. But I assure you it is true and these opportunities are all around us every single day and are accessible. The problem we have is that we have been programmed to only seek income from one source which is the most labor intensive. The rich however rarely ever derive income linearly. In fact, they detest it and reject it. It's like a bad word – a sin, even. They'd much rather work for free and donate the time than to lead some company to falsely believe that it could actually pay them wages once for a task that would pay the employer over and over again. They'd rather volunteer first as many often do. It's just a different mindset altogether and we'd be wise to adopt it. But many of us choose to simply pass over these lucrative opportunities to produce residual and passive income instead of seeking them out and capitalizing upon them.

There is an acronym for the word poor that I have found to be so true. P.O.O.R - **PASSING OVER OPPORTUNITIES REPEATEDLY**!!

A good example of passive income is the guy who owns rental real estate. This guy buys a single family home that was sold under foreclosure for $25,000.00 with an after repair value of $110,000.00. Don't think that's unrealistic because there are cities across the country that you can buy brick houses at this price and all day long – I have done it personally and still do. The investor spends another $10,000.00 in renovations getting the property ready to rent. After doing a market analysis on the rental market in the local area and neighborhood, he found that $850.00 in monthly rent was adequate. Because he had great credit and so much equity, he was able to secure 100% financing for both the purchase as well as the rehab which means he had no money out of pocket in the deal.

Anyway, the $35,000.00 note required a monthly repayment amount with principal, interest, and escrow of only $250.00 a month. You do the math. This simple transaction yields the investor positive cash flow of $600.00 per month every single month for the next 15 years or more. That's $7,200.00 per year without getting out of the bed.

But that's not the half of it. This guy goes out over a 12 month period and buys 6 more homes around the same price range and once again rents them all out for the same amount. Now simple arithmetic will confirm that just by making these strategic moves in real estate, the investor has just created $36,000.00 in annual income or $3,600.00 a month – and doesn't have to get out of the bed. What's more, the tenants in each of the properties are effectively paying off the five houses for the investor! I know, sounds too good to be true right? Remember the total rent is $850.00 so the $250.00 is going toward the principle and interest which means the note will be paid off one day.

Well for the skeptics and critics, this method of creating passive income is a personal favorite of mine. I have been fortunate enough to have purchased many investment homes ranging from 1,200 to 2,200 square feet for as little as $20,000.00, put anywhere from $5,000.00 to $20,000.00 in renovations in the projects and enjoyed rental income of $750.00 to $850.00 per month per unit. Trust me, it works like clock work. It is really not difficult at all to do and absolutely everyone should do it. Well not everyone – after all somebody's gotta pay rent, right? Yeah, somebody does but it doesn't have to be us. Every American should own at least one rental property besides their primary and secondary homes.

Do you realize how many people work and struggle everyday and earn LESS than $36,000.00 per year? Are you kidding me? It's simply because we have been taught to produce income only one way – and that's the hard way.

Finally, we have come to **Portfolio Income**. This method of income is generated from investments, stocks, mutual funds, interest, royalties, I.O.U's, dividends, and capital gains. Here again, these vehicles require no labor whatsoever. With portfolio income, we simply invest a sum of cash and realize a return on the dollar amount invested.

Let's assume we have $10,000.00 to invest and we choose to invest it in a mutual fund which has been averaging over the last 10 years about 15% a year in earnings. Once again, simple mathematics discloses that our $10,000.00 will earn us the sum of $1,500.00 in interest for the year thus turning the initial $10,000.00 into $11,500.00 or $125.00 per month in income.

Listen Folks, for those of us who may not have a lot of money to invest, this is our problem. We look at millionaires who invest the big money such as a million bucks under the same terms and earn $150,000.00 (15%) and turn our noses up at earning only $1,500.00. But we are missing the principle which works on every level from a mere $10.00 all the way up to $10,000,000.00. We have to learn to not despise the days of small beginnings and start to work principles at the stage we are now. Remember, principles are universal and work on every level.

Also, with portfolio income, the investor gets to enjoy a powerful vehicle in wealth building known as compounding interest. Compounding interest is the principle of adding accumulated interest back to the principle amount and enjoying the benefit of earning interest on the combined amount (the interest earned plus the original principle invested). Compounding interest is a rich man's best friend but the poor man's worst enemy simply because he is on the wrong side of the equation.

Let's go back to the example of the $10,000.00 that we have available for investing. Again, our principal amount is $10,000.00. We have found an investment instrument that will yield us 15% APR. This percentage is about the average rate of return that one could reasonably expect to receive from investing in a very good, aggressive growth mutual fund. We all know that 15% of $10,000.00 is $1,500.00. Now what many of us would like to do as soon as we get our hands on $1,500.00 is of course "consume" it or deplete it. But keep in mind we have grown beyond that as we have embraced the financial mindset and wealth principles of this book.

Instead of consuming, depleting, or using it up completely, investors who understand the power of compounding interest know that it is in their best "interest" to reinvest the amount earned along with the original principal. Thus, the next year (could be the next month depending on the compounding frequency) instead of starting out with the original $10,000.00 , we'd be starting out with $11,500.00. And it doesn't take a mathematician to figure that interest applied to $11,500.00 is gonna yield a better payday than if we only invested the original $10,000.00. There's no rocket science here. We're still dealing with arithmetic and that's great because once we get beyond that we're veering beyond my pay grade. Don't laugh because I know people who are proficient in calculus but their broke!

If we took the principal amount of $10,000.00 at 15% and elected to extract the 15% each year for a period of 5 years we would have earned $7,500.00 over 5 years ($1,500 X 5). However, if we reinvested the interest that was earned each year and added to that amount the principal, the amount of interest earned would be $10,113.57. That's an amazing $2,613.57 more or over 26% more than our original principal amount invested. If we elected to merely extract and hold the $1,500.00 earned each year at the end of 5 years we'd have a total of $17,500.00. Not bad, right? However employing the mechanism of compounding interest we would end up with $20,113.57 which is a great deal better. As a general rule, we can always double our money every 5 years with compound interest if the average APR is 15%. The key here is the 15% rate combined with compounding interest. We should always strive to achieve both.

CHAPTER 9

$50,000.00

ANNUAL INCOME

GUARANTEED

FOR ALL!

In this chapter, I want to get straight to the point – some real talk here. It is absolutely no excuse for any American living in the greatest country on the planet to not own his or her own business. Now this includes being apart of a partnership, closely held corporation, informal investment group, and/or multi-level marketing organization. I understand we may make $250K a year or so on our respective jobs and are doing well for ourselves but we're missing the point. That's just enough to take care of our individual households. What about helping someone other than ourselves? What about leaving a legacy or inheritances? What are we going to bequeath? These terms are absolutely foreign to some of us and we assume that I'm speaking in tongues when I talk about these things. To many, it is an unknown language - but it should not be so.

There is absolutely no justification why any healthy American living in this great country is not earning at least $50,000.00 per year. That's right - that means there is no excuse for poverty. You see, I can talk a little rough now that I'm embarking upon the conclusion of the book. Again, there is no excuse for anyone to be earning anywhere near what the US Department of Health and Human Services classifies as poverty level.

Now I disclosed earlier that I am an entrepreneur at heart and fully expect that I will be one until the day they put me in the wooden box. I am a strong advocate of being proactive in creating our own wealth and opportunities opposed to waiting for others to do so for us. Creating and building a small business is one of the best vehicles to accomplish this. And now that we have learned about the different methods of producing income, we can now center our business models around the more efficient ones.

Before learning about Passive and Residual Incomes, we may have started a business without regard to how many times we could get paid off of performing a task once. Now we have a different prospective altogether and are equipped with the proper information to make much wiser choices in deciding which direction to go in or industry to pursue.

For an example, before now we may have been considering opening an auto repair shop where of course we would be the master technician. But now we realize that although we love to fix cars, we will be signing up for spending the next 20 to 30 years trading time for dollars. It is certain that auto technicians can earn very good incomes – I have some good friends who run their own shops. We could clearly net $50,000.00 a year. But again, if we don't go in to work, we don't get paid. There are no paid vacations and more importantly, when we die, so does the income we were producing. Now our sons have to step up and do it all over again. We will be bequeathing more hard work for very little return considering how we could have better invested that precious time.

Many would say, "But Donnie, you don't understand. I love fixing on cars. It's my life's passion." What I'd reply to that person is this – "Okay, well go spend the valuable 8 hours that you'd work so diligently at the service center creating an insurance client base of 158 clients for a year – or two years even. This will pay you $75,000.00

annually without you having to get out of bed like the insurance agent we discussed previously. Then once you have established this income stream in about a year or two, repair cars for free for the next 10 to 20. And again, another disclaimer – the language used in this segment is not meant to discredit in any way the auto repair industry or degrade those who are currently shop owners or those who endeavor to be. Hear my heart here. We just have to approach this money thing a little smarter.

Here is a list of businesses that one may consider which will produce residual or passive income.

1. Life Insurance Agency
2. Automobile Insurance Agency
3. Health Insurance Agency
4. Multi-Level Marketing Sales
5. Phone Service Sales
6. Utility Service Sales

As I promised earlier in the book, I want to take this time to identify 2 different businesses that any regular person earning poverty level income can start and earn $50,000.00 or more their first twelve months in business. Keep in mind now, these businesses do not necessarily represent the highest and best use of one's time but they will transform personal income statements almost immediately.

I agree with my wife, Selma, that it is important to offer various solutions that people can take advantage of immediately. It is very easy to just offer the businesses that bring residual and passive income but I understand that many of those businesses may not be an option for many as some require state and federal licensing. And some people want to just keep it very simple - they don't mind hard work, but just want a simple idea to earn more money coupled with the execution of the other strategies of this book such as saving, budgeting and not being a classic consumer. That's fine and I applaud that – we all have to start somewhere.

The problem I have is with precious people working on a long term basis for minimum wage up to $10.00. We do not have to do that – not in America. That is third world country money when considering the wealth and economy that we enjoy here in the states. We have to change our thinking. There are literally millions of good people in this country who earn below $30,000.00 a year and my goal is to change that and offer real attainable solutions that will transfigure those circumstances - like immediately. I will say it again – nobody living in the United States of America in the 21st century who is reasonably healthy should be earning less than $50,000.00. Period!

Speaking of being healthy, I met a young man the other day as I pulled into a convenient store parking lot who was deaf and holding a sign. The sign read, "I am deaf and need help. Please give a quarter." I took note as I passed him while entering the store to get directions. I couldn't help but notice that he was slim, dressed normal, appeared to be about 38 to 40 years old, about 6 feet tall and from what I could see seemed to be in good physical health. He was sitting on a stoop in front of the store when I pulled up but got up to approach me as I was returning to my car. He had some pep in his step while coming to me but I did notice that he had a speech impediment as he was attempting to read his sign to me.

Now I went ahead and gave the guy the quarter as the sign requested. I would have given much more. However I couldn't help but wonder why his sign read like it did. I am certain that he probably collected $15 to $20 easy per day working the patrons of the convenient store. However if I were him, my sign would read something like this – " I am deaf and am looking for work; please hire me!" I don't mean to be cruel at all but my thought concerning this young man was, "Okay, I understand you're deaf and are unable to speak and I am sorry about that. But you're not LAME! Cut some grass, wash some cars, trim some hedges, sweep the parking lot, pick up some trash, mop some floors, wash some windows. . ." Instead of getting the quarters totalling $15 to $20 a day, he could be getting $100.00 or more.

I told of that account not to pick on the gentleman but to demonstrate the attitude and mindset that many of us display. We often times focus on everything that is wrong with us or on the areas where we are lacking opposed to appreciating and utilizing what is right and focusing on our strengths. We are quick to say, "I can never do that. I can't sell insurance. I can't do multi-level marketing. I am afraid to talk to people. I'm afraid of being rejected." We go on and on and on about what we cannot do instead of making a list and focusing on what we can do.

Therefore for those of us who find ourselves in this category, I am gonna go down a road that we rarely find motivational and self help authors going down. I would like to introduce to you 2 simple businesses that absolutely anybody and everybody can start and earn at least $50,000.00 per year. What's more, launching either of these two businesses would require start-up money of less than $200.00 and can be done in your spare time after you get off from the plantation – I mean job. Now if the person earning $30,000.00 a year or less examines each of these businesses which can be started for under $200.00 and admits that they can in fact do them successfully, but makes the decision to not get started immediately then I would recommend he or she seek psychiatric help promptly.

AUTO DETAILING

The first small business that I would like to introduce is one that every one can partake in and one that will never go out of style. Sophisticated people may refer to it as automobile detailing but the bottom line is that it's "washing cars" – only professionally. Now I know that many of us may feel that we could never do a business like this because it is too labor intensive and somehow beneath us. "I'm a professional," we might say. I can't tell you how many times I've seen professional, P.O.O.R. individuals who earn $18,000.00 a year who **P**ass **O**ver **O**pportunities **R**epeatedly. For those of us who don't know it, $18,000.00 a year is about $9.00 an hour and is not nearly enough to run a household. We're in a lot of trouble if this is the situation we are in and we need to seriously consider an auto detail business and put our egos to the side.

Auto-detailing is a craft that anyone can learn in a relatively short period of time. Please understand that washing a car professionally is a whole lot different than just washing our own cars at home. Many of us, especially ladies, think we've done something magnificent when all we really did was sprayed the car down, dried it off, and put some Armor All on the tires. Folks nobody's gonna pay us to do that- at least not more than once.

Almost everyone I know owns at least one car many of which are fairly new and many pretty fancy. In this day and age, it's all about image and prestige and the average cost for a new car is hovering right around $28,000.00. That's a lot of cheese! Most people who make the decision to pay that kind of money for a car are interested in how they look and keeping that car clean is definitely something they are interested in. Keep in mind we are talking about the average priced car and haven't even gotten into the luxury cars that range from $40,000 to well over $100k. These guys may start out washing the cars when they first get them but the task gets old after about 30 days.

The concept of this business is so simple and income possibilities are so astounding that I am truly amazed that more individuals have not tapped into it. We can really earn $50,000 a year by washing cars. Here's the formula which is not very complex. In fact, I have been trying to think of a way to make it sound more difficult than what it really is and only because I know the mind set that many of us have. If it's too easy, then it can't be real. Anyway, all a person needs to do is find 40 customers who will agree to allowing them to professionally clean their car every week. Or if every week is too frequent, then 80 people twice per month. That's it!

Once again, it all boils down to simple mathematics. If you take 40 customers at $25.00 per wash, that's $1,000.00 per week. Come on, Man! A grand a week working my own schedule and not having the stress of the work place? You've gotta be kidding me!

It gets even simpler than that. We are well aware that most families have more than one nice automobile. The wife would have a nice Acura MDX while the husband would sport an S Class Mercedes – come on, you know the deal. Everybody knows they would love to have someone show up at their home every week to keep those bad boys looking brand new. For one thing, the prestige they'd get from neighbors is worth 50 bucks by itself. Therefore if you can find just 20 select customers who agree to get both cars professionally cleaned once a week, it's a wrap. We've just created a $50,000.00 a year business in our very own neighborhood. Do the math – 20 customers X 2 vehicles X $25 per vehicle = $1,000.00 per week X 50 weeks a year figuring in a two week vacation = $50,000.00.

This is America, Baby! It is the greatest country on planet earth. Now I don't know if this will work in Africa because they may not be as big on spending or consuming as we are over here. But everybody knows I'm right. Blacks, Whites, and Indians alike will pay me $25.00 per car every week to keep their prized possessions looking brand new.

It's a no-brainer! I don't even need a brain for this! I don't need a high school diploma, G.E.D. , PhD, to make this happen for me and my family. I have personally done this business myself and I'm telling you from experience that it works like clock-work.

Just a few things to keep in mind – this is a business and it has to be ran as such. I do not recommend that anyone go out and try to wash anybody's car professionally without some basic training first. I realize that many are excited and feel that anybody can wash a car but that's not true. Hear me out now. This is important and will make things hard on us needlessly if we don't get it right from the start. Keep in mind, I've already experienced it - only I didn't have anyone to advise me of how to avoid costly mistakes.

Take the time to learn from a professional how to properly clean or detail a car first. Cleaning and detailing are two different animals. See there, most people think they are the same but they are very different – about a $75 difference in cost. I advise anyone seriously looking to engage in this business to take a minimum of a couple of days to a week to just observe and learn from someone who does it professionally. Go to a <u>professional</u> detail shop and talk to some of the guys who are really good and get some pointers. Invest $25.00 in getting **your** car washed or $100.00 to get **your** car detailed. Watch how it's done and you will find that you didn't know as much as you thought, nor were you anywhere near as thorough as you thought. But make sure you learn from a true professional who takes pride in his work as there are plenty of sloppy employees who work at these shops who call themselves detailers but are far from it. This is so important because you rarely get a second chance once you do a poor job on somebody's car. Trust me.

STANDARD CAR WASH $25 to $35

1. Thoroughly wash (with liquid soap) the entire car with a sponge including fender wells, tires, and rims.
2. Thoroughly dry entire car with chamois or "shammy."
3. Windows (inside and out) must be streak-free and careful attention should be paid to them. This is where most fail. Use windex and newspaper, or windex and paper towels for best results.
4. Thoroughly remove and discard all obvious trash and wipe down dashboard along with gear console ensuring they are free of dust and other particles. Try to refrain from applying chemical cleaners to vinyls as they could potentially cause damage. Some customers want a vinyl protectant such as armor all applied to dashes for the shine but I never did it unless requested to do so. Any papers or other items that are perceived to have even the least value should be placed neatly in a pile.
5. Vacuum interior thoroughly. Trunk is not vacuumed or cleaned unless directed by customer. Take the time to actually look under each seat front and back. Gather spare change that you are almost certain to find. Remember quarters and dimes are not your tip but here's one – place

the change in an obvious place like a cupholder near armrest.

6. Spray a neutral air freshner on carpet front and rear. This is optional and it should be noted that some customers dislike certain fragrances and some are allergic to others. It may be wise to ask and learn each customer's preference.

7. Apply Armor All or other effective protectants to outside of tires and any black moldings made of plastic. Professionals differ on methods of application. Some prefer spraying it on and allowing it to drip dry. Others prefer to apply it with an applicator or sponge. I prefer the latter method because it eliminates for the most part the problem of armor all blowing back on the lower body of the car when driving at 45 mph or more. I admit that the drip dry method tends to offer the best shine and I use this method in certain instances such as when applying to large tires with letters on them. I never spray when chrome wheels are involved as the spray gets on the chrome and quells the radiance of the wheel. Either way, when I choose to spray, I always use my applicator to lightly smooth down the tire just a touch. This minimizes blow back as well. Also, I generally spray the black material under fender wells.

8. Wipe down door jams. Every jack leg car cleaner misses this small step but it makes a difference as it is the first thing a customer sees when they open the car door.

9. Go back over the car thoroughly inspecting it to make sure it's perfect – that is, if you ever want to get to wash it again!

Don't leave any trash or other debris in the customer's yard or around the car. Make sure the water is turned off and everything is put back the way you found it.

FULL AUTO-DETAIL

1. Complete all steps to the standard car wash.
2. Complete Wax. Use applicator pad instead of cloth. Keep wax off of plastic moldings and other rubber items. Open hood, doors, and trunk where wax tends to build up and remove excess wax.
3. Meticulously clean interior (much more detailed than just dusting dash and console). Watch a professional perform this task.

Now tell me, who can't learn to perfect this art in a relatively short period of time? All it takes is a little practice. A person can practice on their own car or next door neighbor's for free and pick up your first customer in the process.

I want to point out just a few more things before anyone gets started that will certainly streamline success. The key here is to try to maximize efficiency as it is obvious that time is a limited commodity. Therefore I would recommend that the overall goal be to build a solid client base comprised of the least amount of customers and if possible all in the same or nearby subdivisions. And I would prefer to focus on clients who are interested and willing to commit to having at least two cars cleaned every single week.

So notice what just happened here – to effect a $50,000.00 a year salary, we have just cut a significant amount of time, travel, and uncertainty. This is not a realistic expectation to start but once a professional detailer is established and known for impeccable work, he'll have more work than time available in a day to perform it. It is at this point where he would notify his clients that he will be only able to service those who are on an automatic weekly schedule. They will understand this once it is communicated that this business now represents his livelihood. I also recommend giving hints from inception and in conversations in between that this is your ultimate goal so it won't be such a surprise when it is finally announced.

However the detailer is to be no fool, though. If he gets the impression that the majority of his client base is not receptive to the idea and will likely stop catering to him altogether, then of course he needs to govern himself accordingly and just work more numbers. This is just the goal, not the iron fist rule. I can hear some detailers complaining, "Donnie, I tried to do that move you said and lost all of my clients and now I'm back at the local supermarket!" Hey, we've gotta use our noggin here!

Start –Up Kit

1.	A chamois or "shammy"	$15.00
2.	100 Ft water hose w/spray nozzle	30.00
3.	Bottle of liquid wash-n-wax concentrate	10.00
4.	Soft Sponge	4.00
5.	5 Gallon bucket	3.00
6.	Bottle of windex	3.00
7.	Bottle of good liquid wax	8.00
8.	6 pack of cotton applicator pads	5.00
9.	Bottle of neutral air freshner	5.00
10.	Swiss broom	5.00
11.	Portable Vacuum(shop vacuum preferred)	<u>20.00</u>

Be careful about using a customer's lighter. **$108.00**

There we have it. Man, I'm excited all over again! I told my wife, Selma that I wanted to go out in our subdivision and build me a client base of 20 real quick. I know I could have 20 signed up in a week or less. That's amazing to me - $50,000.00 a year just like that! It really is as easy as that but the key is performing a professional job every single time. And whatever you do, please, please, please don't go asking the customers to use their bucket, dish detergent, towels, shammy and vacuum cleaner. It's okay to request to use their water, to start.

Remember though, without the financial principles suggested earlier in the book, a person would do just as well to continue working down at the Burgle Doodle. We have to remember that we cannot consume it all. We know that 35% is gone right off the top. Then there are taxes to think about and supplies. I encourage anyone starting out on this journey to get it right from the start. And please don't quit the regular job until you have gotten well established. Trust me if it's done right, it won't be long. But wisdom is justified of her children.

I can honestly say that I will never live near or beneath the poverty level because if all else fails business wise with me, I can always revert back to my auto detailing business. That's a $50,000.00 a year business all day long. Actually for me at this stage it would be at least double that because I'd hire or partner with two other people to work two other neighborhoods duplicating what I was doing. I'd drum up the business myself, split in half the profits with each partner which would yield $25,000.00 a year each additional partner for a total of an additional $50,000.00 to the one I was earning myself.

The sad part about all this is that a lot of our mind sets are so distorted that there are hundreds of thousands of poor individuals who will read this book and be enlightened by this comprehensive plan along with others that I have laid out, but will make the decision to reject these solutions and continue working a minimum wage job. And it will not be because anyone believes it is unrealistic or feels they can't do it – in fact they'll know they can do it. It's that it is just so much easier to simply go to work and punch the clock everyday opposed to actually applying thought to a simple plan that will almost quadruple their income.

Keep in mind that I still say that even the Car Washing business at an impressive $50,000.00 a year is not the highest and best use of one's time and efforts as it relates to producing income. It is still unilateral or linear in nature – trading time for dollars and performing a task once and getting paid only once.

It's only because I've been on the bottom that I know that sometimes it's hard for those of us who are there to grasp the larger picture of what successful self help authors are trying to get across. A lot of times we are found to be very inspiring to those who subscribe to our concepts but we fail to meet people where they are right now. I have become very sensitive to these concerns and realize that lots of people are simply looking for a life line right this minute and it would be a miracle for them to just get stabilized financially – like in a solution to income that will enable them to just cover rent, utilities, and groceries. For many of us, a simple plan to merely get our heads above water would be major. Then, we could see clearly to take the next step. That is my purpose for laying out these two simple business plans but we have to remember that more income alone will not solve our financial problems. The other principles we discussed earlier are essential because there are those who earn over $200,000.00 who are still suffering like the poor and are in financial crisis.

Again, I want to reiterate that anyone and everyone can do this business and there is a great demand for it. I challenge everyone who is earning $30,000.00 a year or less to make a decision to double your income. Just do it on the side and use about half of proceeds to get your finances in line and put aside the other half (don't consume it all). I'm not trying to sell franchises here. I'm not getting anything out of anybody doing this business besides the satisfaction that I was successful in pulling someone free from the grips of poverty and financial turmoil. It gives me no greater satisfaction than to know that I have been apart of the transformation of a real family's life and apart of the financial rescue team that launches families who were once poor and in despair into wealth so that they, too, can help bring another family up.

THE LAWN CARE BUSINESS

The other business that I would offer for consideration is the Lawn Care business. There are a lot of fancy terms for this business but for fear of confusing anyone like me who likes to keep things simple, we're talking about "cutting grass" here. Now I realize many of us are too cute for this and others have already skipped the car washing section as well as this one thinking to themselves, "There ain't no way in the world I'm washing no cars and I'm certainly not cutting nobody's grass – I hope this guy has got more $50,000.00 a year options than these!"

Well, I am gonna have to go ahead and apologize to those pretty people in this category now because while I know of many other businesses that we could earn and profit good income, these are two that I have personally experienced myself and know are fool proof, if my protocol is followed. I used to be one of those guys who wanted to dress up all the time and be clean cut and professional as it related to my livelihood. I remember not wanting to get dirty and being concerned about my professional image. I don't think anything is wrong with that as long as a person is already producing the income they need to produce dressing in business attire.

Nevertheless earning $10.00 an hour ($20K a year) and being broke all the time in a tailor made suit is not what I would consider a position that I'd feel comfortable boasting about. I'd much rather get dirty during the day and count triple the money in cash in the evening – then come home take a bath and put on my executive clothes and look important amongst my peers. That is, if impressing them is what was meaningful to me.

Besides, we are not really fooling anybody anyhow. Everybody has sense enough to know what kind of pay scale we're on anyway by our positions and the companies we work for. If our friends are earning $60,000.00 a year working at Verizon and we think that us having a shirt and tie on after 6pm causes them to believe that we are earning the same, we are sadly mistaken. As soon as we disclose to them that we are a concierge, it doesn't matter what kind of business suit we have on, they know we are earning a modest income somewhere in the mid twenties - $30,000.00 tops. An Armani or Liz Claiborne business suit is not gonna change that. That's just what your average concierge earns.

Nothwithstanding, our families are suffering financially and socially because we are too concerned about what others think about us. We should be more concerned with attaining financial independence and positioning ourselves to provide the best life we can for our children and others we care about.

Anyway, the lawn care business is one that anyone can be successful in. It doesn't cost a great deal to get started with lawn care but much like auto detailing, it is a craft that must be performed with professionalism. Everybody thinks they can cut grass and they can – but at home on their own lawns. Now there are some people who manicure their own lawns better than professional landscapers. For those of us who may fall into this category, I say start immediately. However for everyone else, I recommend we take the time to learn from a true professional before butchering somebody's lawn and causing enemies. I'm not playing here. People are serious about their lawns and won't take too kindly to some bootleg grass cutter messing it up.

This business should be taken very seriously even though many might feel that it is just a medial task which cannot be done wrong. Those of us who have and maintain beautiful lawns and have had bad experiences with lawn care businesses know exactly what I'm talking about.

Take a week or two to learn from a professional lawn care provider and offer to work for free to learn. He might not let you do much to start for fear that you will mess up something, but nobody turns down free help as long as we're serious about actually helping them and learning the trade.

The first thing I want to point out with this business is that it is for the most part a seasonal business, if it were not already apparent to everyone. Depending on which part of the country we live and the climate that goes along with it, professional lawn care providers have about a 6 to 7 month run usually ranging from mid April to about mid October. It is important for those of us who are starting this business to be aware of this.

Let's look at the math. To professionally cut and trim the average yard on a ¼ of an acre lot costs about $40.00. To earn $50,000.00 annually in this business we would have to divide that amount by the actual number of months we would be expecting work to be available which is only 6 months (26 weeks). Therefore dividing $50,000.00 by approximately 26 weeks equals $1,924 a week in income that has to be generated over the 6 months. So if we take the round number of $2,000.00 a week and divide it by $40.00 per lawn, we find that we need a total client base of 50 customers who agree to receive our lawn care services once per week. I'll be the first to tell you that acquiring a customer base of 50 customers is not a difficult task provided we can meet or exceed the customers' expectations.

Not only is getting 50 customers a reasonable reality, but also the fact that once we get really good at managing them and reach the level of full efficiency, we will find that all 50 customers can be serviced in two to a maximum of 3 days out each week. Thursdays thru Saturdays are usually the days preferred by lawn care providers and home owners alike.

"So wait a minute here, you mean to tell me that a person can earn $50,000.00 a year working only 6 months out of the year and only 3 days out the week?" You've got it! There are professionals who do it effortlessly every year and we look at them as if they were somehow beneath us because they seem to be dirty and working hard every time we encounter them. Well if we see them working every day all day long there is one thing we can count on, and that is they are making a whole lot more than $50,000.00 a year. Also, we know that it is impossible that they are working all year round because 90% of all customers do not maintain winter grass. This means that anywhere from 4 to 6 months out of the year, these lawn care providers are off. While many employees are working their socks off in corporate America year round for peanuts, these guys have made enough cheddar over the summer to hibernate for the winter. This sounds better than the previous business as the auto detailer doesn't have such luxuries.

Pretty impressive right? While we are feeling sorry for them, they are feeling sorry for us that we have no better sense than to work twice as long for a half or third of the pay. But keep in mind though, we do at least get to dress up every day and "LOOK" like we're prosperous. You've gotta be kidding me!

The Basic Lawn Cut

1. Cut grass by push mower or riding mower. Most patrons have come to expect riding mowers but the results are what ultimately matters.

2. Trim sidewalks, curbs, and driveways with weed eater and/or edger. Trim around hedges, trees and any lawn furniture.

3. Blow sidewalks, curbs, and driveways with a blower.

EXTRAS Not Included In Basic Lawn Cut

1. Trimming hedges — $20 to $$35
2. Planting flowers (Labor Only) — $50
3. Cleaning flower beds — $25 to $50
4. Spreading mulch — $25 to $50

The method of building a customer base with this business is much like that of the Auto Detailer. I recommend approaching it strategically with maximum efficiency. Of course we would want to choose a neighborhood or subdivision that boasted 200 or more homes in it to try to concentrate our efforts in one general locale instead of having to run all over the city. Trust me, this can be accomplished between two to three local subdivisions if properly targeted.

Keep in mind though, unlike the mobile detailing business many customers may already have a provider that they have been patronizing. The key here is the results that we are ultimately gonna be able to display. Customers are willing to change if they are given a reason to. Moreover, lawn care providers tend to get complacent, especially after about two seasons and they get used to the money. A lot of customers become dissatisfied but stay with them simply because they've been solicited by no one else. We just have to make sure that we don't fall into this unfortunate group and get cut off as well.

To start this lucrative endeavor, all one would need is the following equipment.

Start Up Equipment

1.	Used Push Mower	$50.00
2.	Used Weed Eater (A good one)	$75.00
3.	Used Blower	<u>$60.00</u>
	Note: Finding these items at a good yard sale will cut this figure in half.	**$185.00**

Wow, indeed this is the greatest country in the world. Now please tell me who could not do this business immediately? And don't say that $185.00 is the hold up. Okay, here's how to handle that. Be creative. Let's use our noggin! Tell a friend, neighbor, or family member what we are endeavoring to do and ask to borrow their equipment for two days. Offer to give them half of the profits – let's not ask them to do it for nothing!

If nobody likes us and we can't get that done let's line up 3 or 4 yards and go rent a push mower and weed eater for $50.00, make $120.00 and then go buy a used push mower with the difference. The next day go rent the weed eater for $25.00 and make another $120.00 – in case we didn't pick up on it we don't need a blower at this point because a broom will do the same job, though we may not look as cute or professional as we do it. Bottom line here is we're in business.

A homeless person can do this business. Come on everybody – we're in America! It is no excuse for anybody healthy to be poor in this country. We need to introduce these businesses to our teenagers, our nieces and nephews. I bet you the young drug dealers on the street never considered they could make this kind of money cutting grass. In fact, most street level drug dealers work more than 40 hours a week and risk years in prison and still don't make this type of money. Instead of just criticizing and ostracizing our youth, present them with some options and alternatives to crime and complacency. Let's get out there and help them establish these businesses and get them off to a good start. They'll take pride in themselves and the business and take it to new heights. We may be too pretty or too dignified for the profession but let's give someone else a chance.

Better yet, buy them the book and let them read it and get inspired themselves. Every at risk youth should be introduced to the businesses and principles in this book. Every individual in prison or on parole should be exposed to these concepts immediately.

CHAPTER 10

PRESIDENT BARACK OBAMA!

I know I keep saying this but it's only because I believe it so passionately -this is indeed the greatest country on the planet earth. It is great and exciting to be living in this historic hour. As I watched the final portion of the first day of the Democratic National Convention, I was in total awe as I witnessed the site of thousands of democrats across the country rally together in support of nominating the nation's first African American President. If only Dr. Martin Luther King, Jr. and all of the rest of the great patriarchs, Black and White alike, were alive to see this day.

What a great country! Even though we have the bitter past of slavery and oppression of Indians and African Americans, today marks a time when America as a whole has shown the world that though it may be imperfect, it is constantly growing and getting better. America demonstrates to the world not only that it is superior in financial and economic opportunity, but also in peace, unity, forgiveness, and HOPE! It just gives you that feeling deep down inside that one cannot ever seem to find the words to adequately describe.

And in observing the tears of joy and appreciation on the faces of White women and choking up of White men, I can credibly say that this was not just a moment for Blacks but America as a whole. This is a time of healing, forgiveness, and brotherhood of all fellow Americans regardless of their ethnicity. Hispanics and Indians, Muslims and Christians alike cannot help but be proud of this country's growth and achievements and have real hope that one day that they too might see a

President who looks like them elected to the oval office. It gives hope to their children that maybe it really is possible.

Families across the globe are no doubt watching this great country in amazement saying, "WOW! How amazing!" I can imagine that the extremist, terrorists, jihadist, and others who may oppose the freedom and opportunity that America represents, are shaking in their boots as America takes another giant step toward reconciliation, unity and opportunity for all.

I can't help but wonder what positive impact we must be making even upon all of them. Certainly many of them can appreciate and admire the determination and fortitude that we display as Americans which is just the opposite of theirs - but more powerful. I wonder if they wish or dream sometimes of what it would be like to be like us. I truly empathize with them and their children because although I realize they are true to their causes, I also know that because they are human beings, there has to lie that same love that comes only from our Father the Creator which he has undoubtedly placed in the heart of every person born into the earth.

These guys were not born terrorists and extremists. They were not born into this earth for the sole purpose of Jihad or being a suicide bomber. Instead, they were bred to be so. I mean, a family cannot look at a precious Arab baby that is just born into the world and say, "Here lies the next great terrorist." No, I would have to take for granted that the Arab mother and family imagines very similar to us that the child is a precious gift from God and wishes hope, peace, and prosperity upon them also. I just can't help but believe that every person regardless of race, religion, or culture wants to get the best out life that it has to offer.

No wonder nearly every person who has had the opportunity to hear of the American way of life longs to come here. Sure, there are other great countries across the globe that provide great lives and opportunity for their people but there is just no place like America.

I recall throughout the primaries where many republicans and others would attempt to paint President Obama and his family as Anti-American. How can that be possible? Sometimes in politics we just go too far in our quest to demonize our opponents and advance our respective candidates of choice. But to propagate that somehow Barack and Michelle Obama are bitter Blacks and unpatriotic, and expect intelligent Americans to buy was obviously going over board.

I remember President Obama responding that of all the things he expected to be accused of, he'd never dreamed that one of them would be that he was unpatriotic and unappreciative of all the liberties and opportunities this country provided to him and his family. I mean, that's not generally one of the things presidential candidates accuse one another of because while each may bring a host of different perspectives and positions on issues with respect to which way they want to lead the country, it's usually a given that each candidate loves and wants the best for America. It was obvious that Obama was blown away by the attempts of any to even remotely suggest otherwise concerning him and his family.

Many of his opponents jumped on the opportunity to paint Obama as Anti-American because of his 20 year membership at Trinity United Church of Christ under the leadership of Dr. Jeremiah Wright. Now I know this is a delicate topic for most regardless of which side of the fence we may be on but I thought it necessary to personally weigh in on the matter.

First let me declare that I do not believe that the Rev. Jeremiah Wright is Anti-American despite his controversial sermons and comments regarding this country. Now I certainly do not agree with all of them but neither do I agree with all of my very own Bishop's (Bishop David L. White, Jr.) opinions on issues that he has openly made known both by way of the pulpit as well as social forums. And it's not to say that either of us is right or wrong about either of those issues because naturally to him he is right and likewise to me, I am. But at the end of the day, it all boils down to a person's own opinion or personal beliefs concerning a thing and those convictions are derived from all sorts of things from personal experience, inside knowledge, or perceived facts whether they be provable or not.

I realize that I just lost a good percentage of the crowd that thought I was half way intelligent at the beginning of the chapter, but I guess I blew it again. I have to speak the truth as I see it and believe it, however.

Dr. Jeremiah Wright is not a "kook" as our favorite newscaster Bill O'Reilly has suggested. That has been our problem. If someone doesn't think like we want them to think, or more significantly, if they don't believe like we believe, we ostracize them and discount them to others as loony. The moment someone says something that the masses don't agree with about America or the war, they are branded an outcast and labeled unpatriotic.

I sincerely believe that this is why America and other Western nations are so hated by many of nations – it's because we feel that we are right all of the time and about everything. We attempt to force what we have set as the standard on the rest of the world.

Now I absolutely agree that we should positively influence the world and make an effort to intervene in situations where there is great oppression and genocide, but we are gonna have to resolve at some point the fact that America does not rule the world. The United States Of America is not the parent to every other nation yet we dictate to them as if they were inferior –as if they were our subjects instead of fellow sovereigns. I'm afraid that in addition to inspiring nations to change and become better, we also provoke them and bring out the very worst in them. I believe that if we are not careful in our war on terror and Al-Qaeda we will be creating more monsters (suicide bombers and extremist) than we could ever hope to prevail against. I am in no wise suggesting that we should negotiate with or compromise with terrorists but I do think it is wise to take inventory and study whether we are creating more than we are defeating.

In the case of Rev. Wright, I completely disagree with the way he was portrayed to Americans by the opponents of the Obama campaign and the media. In effect they took two or three sermons and statements out of thousands preached over a period of 30 years or more and reduced the Reverend down to those select few. Never mind the countless sermons of love and devotion to God, family, and country. No mention whatsoever was made of how he won thousands of disciples to Christ. It was not deemed significant to shine any light on the scores of outreach programs he has established nor the millions of dollars of aid funneled to the communities he serves. The only thing that was important here was magnifying to the world controversial statements he made in disagreement with governmental behavior by this country (whether true or untrue). The context of these statements or sermons were not important nor was there any attempt to try to understand the points Reverend Wright was trying to get across.

Then you take those sermons and comments and couple them with the fact that he was friends with Minister Louis Farrakhan and there we have a blazing hot story of treason. We run the distorted story day in and day out for weeks and months at a time while the victim of this distortion and his family helplessly looks on with no real avenue to combat it. This is the power of media – news stations can package and broadcast any message to the world that they choose for millions of viewers to see and buy in to. The problem is that the only context the viewers really get to see is the one that the news stations project. We all know you can take any one story and easily present it in three lights – positively, negatively, and objectively. The way they are presented is generally the way they are received and the presenters of these stories make the ultimate decision on which way they are gonna portray them.

I was not surprised to learn concerning the Rev. Wright controversy that many of the newscasters when asked, admitted that they had not taken the time to listen to the entire sermons that they were reporting on. Wait a minute, how do you accurately portray a person's character and point of view by statements in a sermon when you haven't even taken the time to hear or view the entire tape. It could be that a person was quoting another person. It could be that the speaker was using sarcasm in one particular statement or contrasting in another. Or it could even be that the speaker meant every word that he or she said because they believed it to be true.

But in any case one would expect that the persons reporting would at least have gathered the full context of the statements by at least listening to the entire tape. I would go so far as to expect that they would also listen to a series of other tapes as well when attempting to accurately characterize a person's statements and character, especially one who is as accomplished as Dr. Jeremiah Wright.

Shamefully, all of his 30 plus years of servitude to God, his family, church, and country was reduced to just a few sound bytes. That's amazing. Well I am certain that we could take some of the most well respected pastors in the country from the most conservative churches in America to the most radical and find controversial statements about a number of different issues including those that criticize this country. I am certain that we can take even America's Church, The Crystal Cathedral's pastors and find some controversial material if we dig deep enough. And I don't think we can get any more American than that, with all due respect.

I certainly know that Bishop David L. White, Jr. who is the senior pastor of the local church I attend has preached some sermons that would certainly be characterized as controversial and I guess if I or any of his other members were running for President, he'd be displaced and villanized as well. It was in a church service during Black History Month that I first learned of the Willie Lynch letters as my pastor was educating the congregation on the history of why many Blacks think the way that we do. If the media were to get a hold of that tape, it would probably make Jeremiah Wright look like the model American. But by no means could a person reasonably take that tape and begin to try to accurately define who Bishop David White is. Certainly though, that tape along with about three other isolated ones that I'm aware of could definitely be used to paint him as Anti-American – that is if you didn't mind reporting on them totally out of context.

But that's how we have isolated other nations, to our detriment. We propagate stories one-sided and so strongly that the victims thereof cannot effectively challenge us nor defend themselves. They do not have the luxury of media prowess at their disposal and can only get their stories across one or two voices at a time – and those voices that hear do not affect those of the masses. In Rev. Wright's case, all those that know him are fully aware that his message was distorted and taken out of context but because his church and congregation does not control a mainstream television and radio outlet, all they could basically do was talk about it amongst themselves. Nevertheless their voices were quickly drowned out by 3 and 4 cycles a day news programs broadcasting the opposite to millions day in and day out.

It is when things like this happen and people and nations feel helpless that we breed extremist. While they do not have television stations, they have learned how to get proper media coverage and that's by blowing things up including themselves. They've decided that if we don't care to engage them in discourse, we would have no choice but to engage them in response to their extreme actions. And while I certainly do not agree with their methods, I do have some idea of their frustrations and desperations.

Has anybody ever thought to inquire as to what it is that these extremist want? Or does anybody care? Not to reduce or compare them to terrorists, but has anyone made an attempt to understand Minister Louis Farrakhan, Rev. Jeremiah Wright, Bishop David L. White, Jr. or Black people in general? It's just too easy to write everybody off as a "kook" and ostracize those who have enough courage to think independently of mainstream America.

Do you really believe that Rev. Wright was praying or hoping that God would DAMN America? The place that he resides with his wife, children, and grandchildren? Really?

I am certain that intelligent people like Barack and Michelle Obama got a whole lot more out of Trinity United Church of Christ besides those few sound bytes that have been played over and over again on cable news stations. And while politicians continue their attempts to swift boat Barack Obama and dupe the American people through mischaracterization and fear tactics, I am proud that America has once again demonstrated that she is much wiser than that. As Barack Obama has repeatedly said during his campaign, "Not this time!" And he was right.

Opponents of Barack Obama have failed to successfully drive a wedge between Obama and Rev. Jeremiah Wright and the Trinity United Church of Christ family. They have ultimately failed to drive a wedge between the First Black Lady and the American people – and they have failed this time to pit the Blacks against the Whites in this election in exchange for a leader who will preside over all the country with the spirit of God and his predecessor the late President John F. Kennedy Jr.

Now I will agree that the media has favored Barack Obama during the primary coverage and it's largely because Obama is a fascinating guy. He's young, handsome, invigorating, and one of the best orators of his time. It's really very difficult not to be captivated by him. I think it is positive news that it is even possible that America can think so favorably about an African American candidate for President. That's a story in itself.

I have to believe that Sean Hannity means well in his attempt to so call balance the coverage of the candidates but Dog – he is just out of control. It is one thing to make an earnest attempt to get out what he believes is the truth about a candidate but it's another when he is intentionally advancing theories that he doesn't believe are true himself, for the sole purpose of getting his guy elected. This is dishonest and a betrayal of the trust that may Americans have in news casters. It is an abuse of power and whereas it appears to be as a sport to him, I truly believe Blacks and objective Whites alike don't find his actions very amusing but offensive.

Here's why - and please hear my heart in this. Sean openly admits that he is a conservative republican extraordinaire. He is pro-republican to the bone and that's fine. I have no issues with that as he has every right to be so and to promote and advance the same. Further Sean had every right to endorse and promote his candidate Senator John McCain as well as contrast fervently why he felt his candidate was the best man for the presidency. He had every right to do so even to the extent of openly criticizing Senator McCain's opponent in character and policy. However I feel he had the right to do it only to the extent that he believed that the rhetoric he was advancing was accurate. I am certain he never actually believed that Barack Obama was a Black Extremist under cover among many other theories he advanced.

Cable news media is a powerful vehicle in the world today and it would behoove African Americans to acquire a network of our very own if we are to be major players in the world of business and politics. We have to understand that networks like MSNBC, CNN, and FOX get paid for reporting, controlling, and funnelling news stories into the world so it's really free for them to tell the world any story that they choose. In fact, advertisers actually pay them to do it in exchange for promoting their products and services through commercial ads. Therefore, Sean promotes negative falsities for 6 months or more straight and actually gets a check for doing so while Obama had to pay $100 Million or more to challenge it with very little hopes of being successful in doing so. What if the Obama campaign owned a major network of its own? I can hear Bill O'Reilly saying, "They do – MSNBC, CNN, CBS and all the rest!" Anyway, we all get the picture here.

I just don't believe, however, that Sean is measuring up to these fundamental standards. Sean has been attempting for months to get the American voters to falsely believe three things regarding Barack Obama that I believe with all my heart that he never believed was true himself. In doing so, he is abusing his power and authority on both cable news as well as radio and basically sold his credibility for ratings. Whether negative or positive, the American people rely upon Sean and other news show host to at the very least advance honest perspectives of candidates. The following are the false messages that Sean Hannity has vigorously promoted:

1. Barack Obama is a Black Extremist. The suggestion here is that because Minister Louis Farrakhan endorsed him and Rev. Wright likes Minister Farrakhan that he must share his views. There must be a conspiracy. Because he is friendly with William Aires, maybe he is a terrorist undercover. Maybe Barack is gonna get together with Rev. Wright and the rest of these guys and attack the U.S. Capitol building or something.

2. Barack Obama is not Pro-American. Fear that Obama has some ulterior motive such as gaining the presidency and putting all the White people out of the country or some similar absurdity. Maybe he's suggesting that Obama is a suicide bomber under cover or something.

3. Michelle Obama is Anti-American and an angry Black Woman. Taking out of context what Michelle said about being proud of her country for the first time in her adult life, Sean suggests that somehow she is bitter and not really for America. Also, because she made a statement about America being a mean country with regard to politics, he suggests that maybe she doesn't think much of America.

The question here is which of these absurdities does Sean Hannity actually believe is true himself? Come on now! They're absurd yet he has no reservation day in and day out promoting them and even making sport of them. If he actually believed the things were true it would be different. But Sean is very intelligent and knows very well they are not true but continues to insult average Americans' intelligence every single day. This is a disgrace and I don't care who the candidate is – whether Senator McCain, Senator Hillary Clinton or Barack Obama. It's just wrong and I believe he will pay a price for it professionally.

I don't have any reservations whatsoever stating publicly that I had no plans of voting for Senator John McCain. I disagreed with quite a few of his positions and simply did not feel he was the best of the two for the job. Nonetheless, I have a tremendous amount of respect for him and his service to our great country. I regard him as an American Hero and a dedicated public servant but I was not gonna vote for him. At the time, I refused to degrade or insult him. I refused to disrespect him or question his patriotism or motives being anything other than what he thinks is best for America. I refuse to allow anyone around me to make fun of his age or advance negative rumors that are unsubstantiated.

In fact, I remember having a discussion with my wife around the time when the news story broke regarding suspicion of Senator McCain having a recent affair or improper relationship with a colleague of his. While I knew I hadn't planned on voting for him either way, I was appalled that they would report such a story with absolutely no evidence of its authenticity. Whether true or false, I feel that it was an unfair attack on our Senator's character, if there was no proof. To this day, I am still unaware of the existence of any proof. This was blatantly unfair to Senator McCain, his wife and family. Now come up with the proof and it's fair game. But until then, it's foul play and an utter disgrace to so disdainfully attack an American War Hero and sitting Senator in the name of politics.

I realize that I'll probably get slammed for this but I'm only saying openly what everybody already knows to be the case anyway. It's just that nobody really has a medium by which they can proclaim it, thus the Seans of the world go unchallenged and their distorted fires go unquenched (I realize it wasn't Sean this time). This is why it is so important for Blacks to own and completely control a major news network. Talking about these issues and discussing them amongst ourselves does not affect the powers that be. Sean doesn't care that the NAACP has this discussion about his unjust tactics because he knows that we do not have a medium to get the message out to anyone besides ourselves. And talking about it amongst ourselves does not affect his world. Now if we could address it on a rival cable news station in prime time, where his Mom, Dad, and colleagues could see it, he'd be very concerned. But we've gotta understand something here, without it it's like we don't exist and can never affect his world.

Black people need to understand these facts. Unless we control major newspapers like the Wall Street Journal, New York Times or a cable news network like CNN or MSNBC where we reach a diverse audience of millions of mainstream Americans, we are locked out of their world. African Americans need to own and control mediums like a Yahoo or Google to be effective. We are simply ill equipped to affect their world with our resources not pooled together.

If Sean Hannity reported for 5 days straight that Donnie Hyder was gay, I don't care what I say or what my momma says or even what my wife says, to the American public Donnie Hyder is Gay! I can get Pastor DeLoyce to announce from the pulpit that I'm not gay and reach several hundred. I can hand out flyers in my community opposing Sean's characterization and reach another couple of hundred. I can even email all of my family and friends and have them to email their family and friends. Still, I haven't even touched a thousand people yet and after watching Sean for 5 days straight, ½ of those in my own camp still will tend to lean toward Sean because of his position and frequency of hammering the story.

With all the tens of millions the Obama campaign raised, they'd spend it all in a week trying to reach the pool of people that Sean has tainted with these falsities. Sean Hannity has been promoting this stuff nonstop for several months now. How could Obama compete? He couldn't. He had no choice but to rely upon the intelligence and the good judgement of decent hard working White American citizens to discern the truth and reflect the same in their voting. He had to rely upon them to vote their hearts and conscience rather than basing their decisions on unfounded fears promoted by Sean Hannity that he himself never believed were true.

Now take for instance Allan Colmes – he gives the liberal perspective on the Hannity and Colmes Show but if you'll notice he tends to be fair with even those he disagrees with. He'll oppose you tenaciously but I have yet to see him viciously attack anyone. He disagreed with Senator McCain on a number of issues and certainly made sure he pointed out his weaknesses but he never appeared to have a personal vendetta against him. I never once heard Allan disrespect the Senator or his family although he did make it his business to let the world know of his flaws, which was fair game.

While I'm at it, I might as well weigh in on Bill O'Reilly. Now I've gotta admit that I really like this guy. He is much more sophisticated than Sean, and Bill does care very much about his image as a reasonably fair news announcer. I have discovered that Bill's approach is two fold and a double edged sword. Bill will speak in hard terms exactly what is on his mind despite what anyone thinks about it, in most instances. But when it comes to sensitive issues such as Barack Obama, I've learned that he takes a different approach in getting his point across – and very effective I might add.

Bill O'Reilly brings guests to his show who are what I call "loaded guns" on the sensitive issues and messages that he wants to get out, but doesn't want to be the actual deliverer of the message himself. In short, he brings people on to say what he doesn't care to say but feels needs to be said. I have studied him night after night and it's like clockwork. I tell my wife the position of the person before they open their mouths and I explain to her what Bill is gonna say in return. He asks them a loaded question knowing that it's gonna set them off in the direction he wants them to go.

Most of the time they go overboard and he steps into the role of referee and calls their position "over the top" so it appears that he is defending the person who was attacked. Therefore Bill gets credit for breaking up the fight that he himself instigated from the start. He gets the principal's award for citizenship for fights that he broke up in the school yard but nobody realizes that he's the one who got the rumors started to begin with. He's the culprit that actually caused the bully to bloody the wimpy kid's nose.

It reminds me of the character in Dora the Explorer known as Swiper the Fox. This character is notorious for being very cunning but Dora and her friends have come to realize his method of operation which currently limits Swiper's ability to be effective. Whenever Dora and the gang suspects that Swiper is up to his tricks they circumvent it by saying, "Swiper no swiping, Swiper no swiping, Swiper no swiping!" If they can say that three times before Swiper the Fox is successful with his plot, then Swiper has to back off and is known for famously responding, "Ahhhhh Man!"

I have found that Dora's number one strategy to combat Swiper the Fox's traps is her vigilance. Therefore, I challenge everyone to study Bill O'Reilly or "<u>Swiper</u> <u>With</u> <u>FOX</u>" and take notice of the way he subtly sets the guests up to attack guests that he disagrees with as he did in Barack Obama's case. I encourage everyone to do like Dora and friends every time they catch him doing it. You've gotta say three times to Bill O'Reilly, "Swiper no swiping, Swiper no swiping, Swiper no swiping!" And after awhile ole <u>Swiper</u> <u>with</u> <u>Fox</u> will have to give it up and say, "Aaaaaaaaah Man!" He'll go back to the drawing board and find another strategy. And I'm not bashing Bill O'Reilly as I'm a fan of his show, but I do applaud Barack Obama and other victims for not letting Bill O'Reilly push them around.

I do however have a few issues to address with the President, though. I encourage you Mr. President to continue to be strong and be the advocate and facilitator of the CHANGE that you promised and that we all so passionately long for. I encourage you to resist the temptation to succumb to the pressures of politics that are sure to confront you. Do justice for all Americans, not just for Blacks yet not excluding Blacks either. Be fair to Whites, Hispanics, Indians and every other American alike as you endeavor to lead and turn this nation around.

America is depending on you to bring us all together in unity. We trust your judgement, your wisdom, and more importantly the fact that you genuinely have this country's best interest at heart. We are confident that you have the ability along with everyone's help to make this country what we all know it can be.

I encourage you to engage the American people openly and honestly about the issue of race so that we can transcend it. We cannot effectively do so if we ignore the issues and pretend they do not exist. America is ready to face these issues head on – we just need the right President to lead us in the journey. We believe and trust that it is you. I realize that it will not be an easy task and will require a lot of guts and tenacity to accomplish it, but this is one of the main reasons America hired you. "Why do you think we hired you?" Never mind the critics and naysayers – history will be the judge.

White people bear with the Obamas. They are not White – they are real Black people. Don't expect them to be playing Mozart in and Cindi Lauper in the White House. I'm telling you now that they're gonna be pumping that T-Pain and Mary J. Blige and Kanye West. But that's okay. He's gonna do a great job for everyone. Don't expect him to walk all geeky and to shake hands like White guys. Barack is real brother but no one to fear – just a little different in culture. But let's appreciate those diversities opposed to being critical of them.

The Obamas' parties are gonna be a little different than the Bush parties. There are probably gonna be soul train lines and of course the electric slide, both old and new versions. Don't trip about it – it's all good.

Now I do agree that Barack shouldn't have old broke down cars and car motors in the back yard of the White House. I do agree that he should continue to tuck his shirt tale in and not wear his suit pants half way his buttocks. I agree that it would probably be unpresidential for Barack to sport gold fronts in his mouth while representing the country and that it probably won't be a good idea to put spinners on Air Force One. I think he should, however, change out the stereo system therein and install some amplifiers and subwoofers so they can crank that Soulja Boy at 35,000 altitude!

I don't expect that Barack will be cashing his check down at the local check cashing joint in D.C.. Michelle much like Selma will make sure he's on direct deposit so no problems there. And I'm certain that Barack is not gonna be requesting an advance on his check every other month either because "The Audacity of Hope" is holding him down and we all know that Michelle has put away some cheese for rough times. So no worries, America, all the ducks are in a row.

But thanks for having enough confidence in him to represent us all as President of the United States of America. Black people have sense enough to know that even if every one of us came out and voted, including our children as well as the million or more Blacks that are incarcerated, we would still come up far short of the numbers needed to elect the first African American President of the United States of America.

I'd like to thank also all the Whites and the families of those who had the judgement and courage to fight for what was right during the Civil War. I am convinced that the children of those freedom fighters are overwhelmingly the ones standing up again in this historic era. America is on a monumental course of change and the new generation is simply tired of the past – the old way of thinking which included exclusion, racism, and bigotry. Those who are still caught up in that era will soon find that they in the minority as we all seek to come together in unity and resolve to the world once and for all that we are in fact truly the greatest country on the face of the earth.

EPILOGUE

I'd like to take this time to thank everyone for reading this book. I sincerely hope that it has been a worthwhile read and will serve the purpose for which it was written – that is to inspire and give hope to those who have lost it. And just as significant, I endeavored to offer practical solutions to everyday problems that each of us face when we wake up every morning.

I encourage every American to rise up and seize the opportunities that this great country makes available to us, especially African Americans.

My prayer is that White Folks were not offended but understand where I'm coming from. Undoubtedly many will seek to attack my message as divisive and racist, but my prayer is that everyone will look beyond just the mere words and see my heart. I am an imperfect individual and do not proclaim to have all the answers but I do care enough about this country to at least attempt to make a difference and make a contribution to society through this earnest writing.

My next book will be strictly a financial one. I did not get the opportunity as I expected to go into detail about corporations, wills, Taxes, Stocks, securities, civil litigation as well as a host of other different topics. I have such a great deal to share regarding my past and present business experiences – my personal failures and successes. I am eager to share how anyone can clear a couple hundred thousand dollars their very first year through very simple real estate investing without any capital or credit. I made catastrophic mistakes and bad decisions largely due to ignorance and fear that I am confident I will be successful in helping many others to avoid the same.

So stay tuned for my next book. I trust it will be even more invigorating and informative than this one which will assist every American in living up to their fullest potential. God bless!

.   http://www.leavewhitefolksalone.com